W9-BYU-228

✳ INSIGHT POCKET GUIDE

COSTA RICA

Discovery CHANNEL

APA PUBLICATIONS

Part of the Langenscheidt Publishing Group

4

introduction

Welcome

This guidebook combines the interests and enthusiasms of two of the world's best-known information providers: Insight Guides, who have set the standard for visual travel guides since 1970, and Discovery Channel, the world's premier source of non-fiction television programming.

To this end it brings you the best of the Central American country of Costa Rica in a series of tailor-made itineraries compiled by Insight's expert on the region, Dona Haber, who has been visiting the country for many years, often for months at a time. The 15 itineraries are divided into five key areas: the first five are based on San José and the Central Valley region, tours 6–8 focus on the Caribbean coast, 9 and 10 explore the Central Pacific beaches, 11–13 cover the country's south, and 14 and 15 link the highlights of the north. Each itinerary includes tips on where to eat and stay along the way, and supporting the itineraries are sections on history and culture, shopping, eating out, outdoor sports and activities, and a fact-packed travel tips section that will help you sort out the practical details of your trip; the latter section also includes advice on the best way of seeing the wildlife.

 Dona Haber has been visiting Costa Rica for many years. Drawn back time after time to this beautiful country, she always finds something new as she renews her acquaintance with people and places. Though one of the smallest nations in Latin America, Costa Rica has a great deal to see and is an extremely rewarding country to visit. The cool cloud forests, idyllic beaches, majestic rainforest, steamy banana plantations and verdant pastures are all there to be explored, along with a remarkable range of wildlife. It is a land of friendly, laid-back people, known as 'Ticos,' of pulsating music and exotic food, and also one of the most peaceful and democratic countries in the region. The capital, San José, is a modern, bustling metropolis while historic Heredia is a colonial city surrounded by lush coffee plantations.

In this guidebook, Dona Haber helps you to sample all these different landscapes and aspects of Costa Rica, along with the simple, everyday pleasures of eating in small neighborhood cafes and buying fresh local produce at road-side stands.

contents

Pages 2/3: Quepos port
Pages 8/9: encounter at a rodeo

History & Culture

Costa Rica is a small, democratic, and peaceful country sandwiched between Nicaragua and Panamá in the Central American isthmus. It occupies less than 52,000 sq km (20,000 sq miles), and is stunningly beautiful and diverse, perhaps more so than any other country of comparable size. Located in the middle of a narrow strip of land known for its political and economic strife, and for its wars, military figures and dictators, the country has flourished as a peaceful democracy for more than 50 years. It was in 1949 that José (Don Pepé) Figueres established a new constitution and rid the nation of the military's overweening influence. Costa Rica has one of the highest literacy rates in the Americas and ranks near the Western nations in terms of the standard of its health care.

When Christopher Columbus landed on Costa Rica's Caribbean coast in 1502, the country was populated by diverse peoples with distinct languages and cultures. Influenced by some of the other indigenous cultures of the Americas, the natives of Costa Rica were skilled in the arts of ceramics, gold- and metal-work, weaving and stone-carving. Costa Rica, it seems, was a mercantile and cultural crossroads of the Americas. Columbus and his successors were particularly taken by the gold that gleamed from the Amerindians' armbands, collars, bracelets, beads and bells, and by the local legends about great gold mines to the south. Today you can see golden artifacts at the pre-Columbian gold museum in San José.

The Rich Coast

Full of great expectations, Columbus named this newly discovered place the Costa Rica de Veragua (Rich Coast of Veragua). As it turned out, ironically and tragically, Costa Rica was to become the poorest and most ignored of Spain's Central American colonies. Costa Rica was not won without a struggle. Expeditions of settlers were defeated over and over again by the jungles, swamps, mountains, heat and rain, as well as by their own bungling and feuding, and the resistance of the indigenous people. In other parts of Central America, native people lived in centralized, highly populated communities. The Spaniards conquered these communities with ease, subjugating and enslaving great numbers of indigenous peoples in the name of colony-building. The ancient inhabitants of Costa Rica, however, lived in smaller, decentralized settlements dispersed throughout the country, which made their capture and enslavement more problematic.

By the time of the development of the Costa Rican colony, the Spaniards had revised some of their more brutal policies, such as *requerimiento* (by which they killed inhabitants who refused to be baptized) and *encomienda* (enslavement of the natives). Thus the

Left: a ceremonial polychrome vessel
Right: a pre-Columbian figure

indigenous peoples of Costa Rica were not enslaved in large numbers by the Spaniards. But they did suffer heavy casualties as a result of their encounters with the colonists. Many succumbed to European diseases, while untold numbers fled to the mountains of Talamanca.

The first attempt, by Don Juan de Cavallón in 1561, to establish a settlement, did not meet with much success, not least owing to a shortage of resources. The slave-labor force was limited and whatever gold there had been was gone – plundered by the early conquistadors. There was little Spanish currency and apparently no simple way to generate more. Most settler families lived on isolated farms in the Central Valley in a state of grim poverty. Their penury was such that even proper clothing was beyond their means. Dressed in simple garments made of goat hair and tree bark, they had nothing to wear to church. So, despite their religious conviction, they could not even attend Sunday Mass. Cacao beans became an informal currency and agricultural techniques learned from the locals became the Europeans' modus operandi.

Cartago, the First Settlement

Colonial communities were slowly growing in the Central Valley. In 1563 the governor of Garcimuñoz (originally near Santa Ana) moved the settlers eastward to what is known today as Cartago, where they established the first permanent Spanish settlement. The village of Cubujuqui, which later became Heredia, was founded in 1706; Villa Nueva de la Boca del Monte (today San José) in 1737; and Villa Hermosa (now Alajuela) in 1782.

Some historians point to this period as the genesis of Costa Ricans' attachment to freedom, peace and independence. They trace the nation's democratic traditions back to those independent farmers who worked their own plots of land in the hills of the Central Valley. Even the colony's governor, so the story goes, pitched in, 'lowering his head to the sun and dirtying his hands' working his own fields. While this analysis may be based more on myth than fact, it does provide insight into the way Costa Ricans live. Today the hillsides of the Central Valley support innumerable modest, lovingly tended houses owned by the

Above: Don Juan de Cavallón
Left: indigenous inhabitants

occupants. Such home ownership by the peasantry is rare in Central America, where the disparity between poor tenants and rich landlords tends to be vast.

Costa Ricans remained largely unaffected by the conflicts that led to Central America's struggle for independence from Spain. Indeed it was a courier on muleback who arrived with the news of Costa Rica's independence on October 13, 1821, one month after colonial officials in Guatemala had declared that country's independence from the faltering Spanish Empire. In Costa Rica this historic development was greeted with ambivalence and confusion. When the dust settled, a schoolteacher, Juan Mora Fernández, was elected the first head of state. Before long, the planting of coffee trees in the Central Valley became instrumental in establishing the country's prosperity.

The Golden Bean

Coffee, the golden bean or *grano de oro*, transformed the economy of the Central Valley from bare subsistence to one of international renown. In the early years of the 19th century, coffee seeds were imported to the New World from Ethiopia and Arabia. By 1840, coffee production had become Costa Rica's foremost industry and the country, with a population of only 80,000, was established as the most prosperous part of the isthmus. San José, boosted by the profits of its coffee exports, became the third city in the world to introduce public electric lighting and one of the first to enjoy the communication

benefits of public telephones. Luxurious private residences, schools, banks, parks and plazas were constructed throughout the city. The Teatro Nacional (National Theater), San José's most glorious building, was specifically built by the ruling coffee barons as a venue for a renowned Italian diva who was touring Central America. Construction was funded by a tax on coffee.

Until 1870, the humid, swamp-infested Caribbean coast area was populated only by a few migrant fishing communities. But as the coffee trade developed, a port with access to the Atlantic was needed for the export of coffee to Europe. El Limón, a fishermen's village of five huts, was chosen. In the same year, the government signed a contract for the construction of the Atlantic railroad from San José to the new port of Limón.

Laborers from as far afield as Jamaica, Italy and China were brought in to construct the railroad. The relentless heat and malarial swamps made for harsh working conditions. Minor Keith, the American magnate responsible for building the railroad, began cultivating bananas alongside the tracks to raise additional funds for the project. Limón thus became a port and a banana town, populated largely by Afro-Caribbean and Chinese immigrants.

Since 1872, Limón and the banana industry have experienced great booms and busts: bumper banana crops have exceeded the value of the country's coffee exports; conversely, labor problems have resulted in a number of violent strikes. After one notorious period of unemployment in the local

Right: coffee beans transformed the economy

industry, Keith's United Fruit Company abandoned the Caribbean coast altogether. As for the railroad, which became known as the Jungle Train, it served communities stretching all the way from San José to Puerto Limón for 100 years. It finally closed down in 1990, owing to serious financial losses and severe and continuous earthquake damage to the tracks.

In 1889 a new constitution promised presidential elections every four years. At this time Costa Rica was a prosperous, politically stable country.

But as the newly generated wealth remained concentrated in the hands of a powerful elite class, the nation's politics became polarized. In response to reformist demands for greater equality, reactionaries were prepared to fight, literally, in defense of the status quo.

Joining the Allies

The reformists found their champion in Dr Rafael Angel Calderón Guardia, who was elected president with more than 80 percent of the vote in 1939. He appeared to be just the man to lead Costa Rica into an era of social and economic reform, but he soon alienated the ruling coffee oligarchy. After the Japanese attack on Pearl Harbor, he declared war on Germany and used his emergency powers of war to confiscate the property of German families, some of whom had not only lived in Costa Rica for several generations but were also connected through business and marriage to the coffee barons.

In 1942 a German submarine sank the *San Pablo*, a United Fruit Company vessel, in Puerto Limón. Calderón's response was to imprison Germans and Italians in the coastal region. Anti-German riots led to the breakdown of law and order, for which José Figueres blamed Calderón. Figueres purchased air time on Radio América Latina and in mocking tones denounced Calderón and his administration. The head of the police force hauled him away in

mid-sentence. Figueres spent the next two years in exile in Mexico but he had already established a heroic reputation among many of his compatriots.

The corrupt presidential election of 1944, which elected Teodoro Picado, was the final straw for Figueres. Now advocating revolution as a means to reform Costa Rica, he set about forming alliances with other nations, stockpiling arms and waiting for the time to strike.

In 1948 Otilio Ulate, publisher of the *Diario de Costa Rica* newspaper, won the presidential election by a large margin but the *calderonista* followers of

Above: today Puerto Limón is a bustling center
Right: three-time national leader José Figueres

Calderón and Picado retained power in congress. Amid charges and counter charges of fraud and ballot papers set ablaze, Ulate was arrested by Picado's police colonel, and his closest advisor, Carlos Luis Valverde, was shot dead.

The ensuing civil war consisted of a well-planned, if somewhat lucky offensive carried out by men with no military backgrounds against a president who had no heart for conflict. Figueres's National Liberation Army emerged victorious and its leader entered San José five days after the ceasefire at the head of a triumphant parade. Echoing the 19th-century English utilitarian philosopher John Stuart Mill, Figueres promised to promote the greatest good for the greatest number. In the course of his short tenure as leader of the junta, or the Second Republic as he called the new order, Figueres enacted sweeping economic and social reforms.

Abolition of the Military

Figueres's expansion of the social-security system involved legislation on child support and low-cost health services for all. He inaugurated a minimum wage, nationalized every bank and extended the franchise to women. Most significantly, he conferred citizenship on everyone born in Costa Rica, including the Afro-Caribbeans of the coastal region, who up till then had been treated as second-class citizens. For many, however, Figueres's most celebrated achievement was the abolition of the military. In a public ceremony, he presented the keys of the Bella Vista military fortress to the minister of public education and struck a sledgehammer against the fortress wall.

On November 9, 1949, Figueres voluntarily ceded power to Otilio Ulate. However, Figueres later served two futher terms as president, 1953–8 and 1970–74. Perhaps his most abiding legacy is the tradition of the National Liberation Party, which he founded. His successors as its leader have included Oscar Arias, who, in 1987, was awarded the Nobel Peace Prize for his courageous efforts to bring peace to Central America.

Calderón's son, Rafael Angel Calderón Fournier, served a lackluster term

Above: local militias featured prominently in the country's civil war

(1990–94) as president, and in 1994, Figueres' son, José María Figueres, was elected in his place. The young Figueres, who grappled with the country's national debt and the privatization of many of the industries once nationalized by his father, became one of Costa Rica's most unpopular leaders. The 1998 elections were won by the Partido Unidad Social Cristiana, whose leader, Miguel Angel Rodríguez, announced his commitment to women's rights, the poor and the young. A conservative economist, he tried to implement a tough austerity program, while awarding himself a fourfold pay rise. Despite encouraging foreign investment and signing free-trade deals with Mexico and Canada, many Costa Ricans were suspicious of his privatization plans for state companies. His government was accused of corruption and lack of transparency, triggering nationwide protests and a general strike in 2000. In April 2002 the PUSC regained power after Abel Pacheco won the first-ever presidential run-off vote. He pledged to overcome poverty and prioritize tourism, but his term has been marked by scandals. Rodríguez went on to become secretary general of the Organization of American States, the first Central American ever elected to head the OAS.

In 1979 the right-wing Somoza regime in Nicaragua was overthrown by Sandinista rebels. On the insistence of the USA, to which it was financially indebted, Costa Rica became a haven for the Contras (anti-Sandinistas). Since 1997, when the USA introduced harsher immigration laws, Costa Rica's role as a refuge for Central American immigrants has become even more pronounced – it is estimated that there are 1 million Nicaraguans in the country. Many of the 'Nicas' escaped the aftermath of the drought caused by El Niño, and the terrible damage caused by Hurricane Mitch in 1998. Countless others were persuaded to leave by Nicaragua's abysmal economic conditions – a staggering 50 percent unemployment and a GDP (gross domestic product) that is only a fraction of Costa Rica's. Refugees also arrived from El Salvador, Honduras and Guatemala, all of which were undergoing varying levels of civil conflict. There have been inevitable problems in absorbing so many newcomers but in general the country has dealt with the situation with a combination of grace and tolerance.

Economic Factors

By 1989 Costa Rica's national debt had reached US$5 billion, forcing President Arias to negotiate millions of dollars of US aid. In recent years, tourism, along with computer chips, have overtaken bananas and coffee as the most important sector of the local economy. Since the mid-1980s visitor figures have risen from fewer than 400,000 to almost 2 million per year. The adverse effects of so many visitors on the country's biodiversity and natural beauty have been debated at length and the country is still trying to balance the competing forces of tourism with the rights of local people and wildlife.

Above: flying the national flag

HISTORY HIGHLIGHTS

40,000–4000BC Hunter-gatherers on the American continent drift southward, settling in small chiefdoms.

4000–1000BC Cultivation of crops such as yucca, maize and cotton.

1000BC–AD1500 Development of permanent agricultural communities.

1502 Columbus lands on a stretch of Atlantic Coast which he names Costa Rica de (Rich Coast of) Veragua.

1519–60 Spanish conquistadors reach both of Costa Rica's coastlines.

1561 Juan de Cavallón establishes Costa Rica's first permanent community, which later becomes the city of Cartago.

1660–70 Cacao beans bring the colony its first revenue but the plantations are subject to pirate raids.

1723–82 Cubujuqui (Heredia), Villa Nueva de la Boca del Monte (San José), and Villa Hermosa (Alajuela) are founded.

1821 Central American colonies win independence from Spain.

1824 The residents of Guanacaste vote to secede from Nicaragua and become part of Costa Rica.

1838 Republic of Costa Rica established.

1840s Coffee becomes big business.

1871 Work is begun on the Atlantic Railroad, linking San José with the Caribbean Coast.

1889 Costa Rica's liberal constitution establishes quadrennial elections.

1890 Completion of Atlantic Railroad.

1897 Inauguration of National Theater.

1934 Banana plantation workers strike against the United Fruit Company and win concessions including wage guarantees and the right to organize.

1939 Dr Rafael Angel Calderón Guardia is elected president and begins to implement social reforms.

1941 Following the attack on Pearl Harbor, Costa Rica declares war on Germany, Italy, and Japan, a day before the United States enters World War II.

1944–8 Fraudulent presidential elections keep *calderonistas* in power.

1948 The National War of Liberation is won by the forces of José (Pepé) Figueres.

1948–9 Figueres establishes a democratic constitution and institutes widespread social reforms, including the abolition of the military.

1949 Figueres voluntarily relinquishes power to the winner of the presidential election of 1948, Otilio Ulate, but later serves two further terms as president.

1969 Santa Rosa National Park is established.

1979 Civil war begins in neighboring Nicaragua, and Costa Rica accepts numerous refugees.

1982 Inflation reaches 90 percent.

1987 President Oscar Arias is awarded the Nobel Peace Prize for his attempts to bring peace to Central America.

1990 José (Pepé) Figueres dies. The Atlantic Railroad closes.

1990–94 Rafael Angel Calderón Fournier, the son of Dr Rafael Angel Calderón Guardia, serves as president of Costa Rica.

1991 An earthquake in Limón province kills 60 people.

1994 José María Figueres, the son of José Figueres, becomes the country's youngest president at 39, and one of Costa Rica's most unpopular leaders.

1996 Swimmer Claudia Poll wins Costa Rica's first Olympic gold medal.

1998 Partido Unión Social Cristiana wins general election.

2000 A general strike and protests against proposed privatization of national telephone and power company.

2002 Abel Pacheco of the PUSC wins first ever presidential run-off vote.

2004 Former president Miguel Angel Rodríguez elected Secretary General of the Organization of American States.

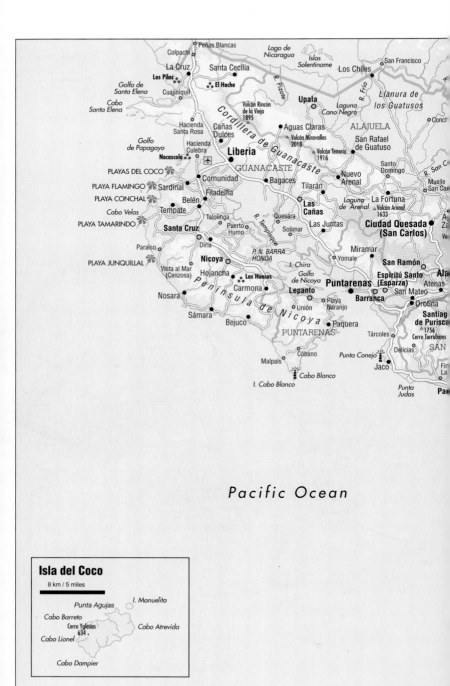

Peñas Blancas
Colpachi
Lago de Nicaragua
Islas Solentiname
San Francisco
La Cruz
Santa Cecília
Los Chiles
Golfo de Santa Elena
Las Pilas
Cuajiniquil
El Hacha
R. Pizole
Upala
Llanura de los Guatusos
Conch
Cabo Santa Elena
Volcán Rincón de la Vieja 1895
Laguna Caño Negro
R. Frío
ALAJUELA
Hacienda Santa Rosa
Cañas Dulces
Aguas Claras
San Rafael de Guatuso
Golfo de Papagayo
Volcán Miravalles 2018
Hacienda Culebra
Nacascolo
Liberia
Volcán Tenorio 1916
Santo Domingo
San
PLAYAS DEL COCO
GUANACASTE
Comunidad
Bagaces
Nuevo Arenal
Muelle San Car
R. San
PLAYA FLAMINGO
Sardinal
Filadelfia
Tilarán
La Fortuna
PLAYA CONCHAL
Belén
Las Cañas
Laguna de Arenal
Volcán Arenal 1633
Cabo Velas
Tempate
Talolinga
Quesara
Ciudad Quesada (San Carlos)
PLAYA TAMARINDO
Santa Cruz
Puerto Humo
R. Tempisque
Solimar
Las Juntas
Za
Vo
Paraíso
Diriá
P. N. BARRA HONDA
Miramar
PLAYA JUNQUILLAL
Nicoya
Vista al Mar (Cenzosa)
Hojancha
Las Huacas
I. Chira
Golfo de Nicoya
Yomale
San Ramón
Ala
Carmona
Espiritú Santo (Esparza)
Atenas
Nosara
Unión
Lepanto
Playa Naranjo
Barranca
San Mateo
Orotina
Sámara
Bejuco
Paquera
Santiag de Purisca
1756
Cerro Turrubares
SAN
PUNTARENAS
Tárcoles
Delicias
Cóbano
Punta Conejo
Jaco
Fir
La
Malpaís
Cabo Blanco
I. Cabo Blanco
Punta Judas
Pa

Pacific Ocean

Isla del Coco

8 km / 5 miles

Punta Agujas
I. Manuelita
Cabo Barreto
Cerro Yglesias 634
Cabo Atrevida
Cabo Lionel
Cabo Dampier

Costa Rica

30 km / 20 miles

Caribbean Sea

ARAGUA

R. Indio

ra de
arlos
gola

Barra del Colorado

Puerto Viejo
de Sarapiquí
a Virgen **Las**
Horquetas
REDIA
Rita

Canta Gallo
Tortuguero

LIMÓN

Cariari

R. Chirripó

Parismina

Roxana
Río Jiménez
Boca
Río Matina

Guácimo
R. Pacuare

Carrillo **Guápiles**

Siquirres
Matina

06
Borva
a

SAN JOSÉ
Monumento
Nacional Guayabo
Strafford

Desamparados
Cartago
Turrialba

Aserrí
Moravia
de Chirripó

nacio
osta
Orosí
Platanillo
Petróleo

Puerto
Limón
Shipwreck
Fenix
★Columbus Landing
September 18th, 1502

Cañon
CARTAGO

San Pablo
de León Cortés
Villa Mills

Penshurst
Punta Cahuita

Cahuita
Puert Viejo de
Talamanca
Punta Uva
Punta Mona

Cerro División
3510
Cerro Chirripó
3819△

LIMÓN
Bribrí
Shiroles
Manzanillo

os
Savegre
La Ese

San Isidro
de El General
3078
Cerro Utyum

R. Sixaola
Sixaola
Changuinola

I. Colón
Archipiélago del
Bocas del Toro

I. Bastimentos

R. Teribé

Barú
Juntas
R. General
Volcán
Buenos
Aires
Cerro Kamúk
3549△

Almirante
I. Cristóbal
I. Popa

Dominical
Pejibaye
Cerro Fábrega
3336△

Punta Uvita
Valle de
El General
Potrero
Grande
Cerro Bine
3204△

Tortuga Abajo
Palmar
Norte
Boruca

Valle de
Coto Brus
Alturas

Bahía
de
Coronado
Cortés
Palmar Sur
R. Gr. de Térraba

Jabillo **San**
Vito
Chiriquí
Grande

PUNTARENAS
Limoncito
Río Sereno

Valle de Diquís
Chacarita
Wilson
Botanical
Gardens ★
Sabalito
Cañas Gordas
Boquete

Isla del Caño
Drake
Rincón
Golfo
Dulce
Ciudad Neily
PANAMÁ

Bahía
Drake
Stone Spheres

Punta Llorona
Golfito
Paso
Pañoas
La Concepción
Gualaca

P.N. CORCOVADO
Puerto
Jiménez
Zancudo
La Cuesta
Santo
Domingo
David

Punta
Salsipuedes
Agua Buena
Bahía
Pavón

Chiriquí
R. Chiriquí

Pótreros
Horconcitos

Península
de
Burica
Puerto
Armuelles
I. Sevilla
I. Boca Brava

Bahía
de
Charco Azúl

Isla Burica Punta Burica

The **Central Valley**

T he sheer diversity of Costa Rica's topography gives the impression of a country far larger than this small Central American territory. There are four major mountain ranges and innumerable rivers and waterways. The land, which rises from sea level to 3,800 meters (12,500ft), stretches from 220km (135 miles) of Caribbean coastline to 1,100km (630 miles) of seashore on the Pacific coast. Yet the country's landmass of 52,000 sq km (20,000 sq miles) is about the size of the state of West Virginia.

The country can be easily divided into the following regions: the Central Valley, the Caribbean (Atlantic) coastline, the more developed central Pacific coast, the remote southern zone and the lush northern region.

The Central Valley *(Valle Central)*, or Central Plateau *(Meseta Central)* as it is frequently called, is the heart of Costa Rica. Two major mountain ranges meet here in an area of only 24km (15 miles) by 64km (40 miles) that is characterized by rich, green volcanic hills and river-filled valleys presided over by three volcanoes and an expansive skyline. The people tend to be friendly, dignified and independent. Some 60 percent of the population lives in the Central Valley – in the congested capital of San José, the major cities of Alajuela, Cartago and Heredia, and in myriad mountain villages and small towns that are scattered through these verdant highlands.

Sweetly Scented Air

The seat of government, the agricultural and commercial centers, coffee farms, churches, theaters, art galleries, casinos, restaurants and universities are all concentrated in this 960-sq-km (600-sq-mile) area. The land rises from 800 meters (2,600ft) to 1,500 meters (4,900ft), and a wonderful climate features temperatures that are usually around 25°C (in the mid-70s°F). The air in the varied, beautiful countryside is soft and sweetly scented.

The following itineraries suggest ways to organize trips into the lush hills of the Central Valley, taking in coffee plantations, colonial towns and churches, orchid gardens, volcanoes (both active and dormant) and national parks. There are opportunities for whitewater rafting on the Pacuare River and experiencing the cosmopolitan delights of San José before heading off to explore the country's more remote regions.

To help you navigate your way around, there are tips on renting a car, hiring a bilingual driver and reserving a tour through one of the many excellent local operators. Taxis provide a good, inexpensive way to travel, and buses go everywhere *(see Practical Information, page 79)*.

Left and **Right:** waterfalls and often-active volcanoes are dramatic features of the Central Valley region

1. DOWNTOWN SAN JOSÉ *(see map, p4)*

This one-day itinerary is best done on a bustling weekday (other than Monday, when many museums are closed). Visit the National Museum, lunch in the café of the historic National Theater and check out the pre-Columbian Gold Museum. Relax on a Gran Hotel terrace, explore the National Art Museum and take a late-afternoon stroll in La Sabana Park.

As is the case in any foreign place, it is a good idea to familiarize yourself with the city (best done with the map that accompanies this book) before you head for the streets. San José is organized on a grid system of numbered streets *(calles)* and avenues *(avenidas)*. *Calles* run north to south, *avenidas* east to west. Southern avenues and western streets have even numbers, northern avenues and eastern streets odd numbers.

Buildings are not numbered and, for the most part, only in downtown San José do streets have names. Hence the address of the Catedral Metropolitana (Metropolitan Cathedral) is Calle Central, Avenida 2–4, which means that the cathedral is on Calle Central between *avenidas* 2 and 4. But it is more common to give addresses in terms of distance in meters *(metros)* north, south, east or west from landmarks, some of which, confusingly, no longer exist. Even the locals perpetually stop one another on the street to ask for directions. They seem to enjoy the interaction and are almost always helpful. Even if you don't speak Spanish, you can generally get a friendly pointer.

Though Costa Rica is, in general, a safe country, theft is a growing problem, especially in San José. The best way to have a hassle-free day is to travel light. Carry a copy of the front pages and the entrance stamp page of your passport and only as much cash as you will need. Use a money belt and leave your wallet, as well as your backpack and valuables, at the hotel. Ask the hotel to call a taxi for you or, if you are feeling more adventurous, ask how to get a bus to the Museo Nacional.

National Museum

The **Museo Nacional** (National Museum; Tues–Sat 8.30am–4.30pm, Sun and holidays 9am–4pm; tel: 257-1433; admission charge) is on Calle 17,

between Avenida 2 and Avenida Central. This is the former Bella Vista fortress where, in 1949, José Figueres announced the abolition of the military and dealt a symbolic blow to the wall with a sledgehammer. The bullet holes in the walls date from the civil war. The museum has a notable collection of pre-Columbian ceramics, natural history exhibits and interesting items from the colonial era.

As you leave the museum, turn left on Calle 17, walk half a block along the cobblestoned, palm-lined pedestrian path and turn left again on

Left: San José. **Above Right:** Museo Nacional. **Right:** Teatro Nacional ceiling

Avenida Central. Head west down the hill to the Plaza de la Democracia (Democracy Square), just below the museum. You may want to browse through the stands of the open-air artisans' market in the plaza. Then continue on foot along Avenida Central for five more blocks and you will find yourself in the middle of the pedestrian walkway, standing near a fountain. The entrance to the **Teatro Nacional** (National Theater) is one block over, on Avenida 2. The café here, a cool and quiet oasis with marble-top tables, ceiling paintings and views out onto the Plaza de la Cultura, is ideal for lunch (closed Sundays). The desserts are especially good.

Theater Fit for a Diva

After lunch, take a stroll around the theater (tours daily; admission charge), which has an interesting history. In 1894 it was hoped that the world-renowned diva Adelina Patti would perform in Costa Rica while on tour in Central America. But she refused on the grounds that there was no appropriate venue. So a coffee tax was imposed to finance the construction of the Teatro Nacional, which was completed in 1897 and inaugurated with a performance of Gounod's *Faust*. Modeled on Paris's grand Opera Garnier, it has an opulent red velvet and gold interior. If you want to see a show here, check the program of upcoming productions on your way out of the theater.

For an understanding of the gold fever that consumed Columbus and the Spanish conquistadors, visit the nearby **Museo de Oro** (Gold Museum; Tues–Sun 10am–4.30pm; tel: 243-4202; admission charge). To get there, turn right as you exit the Teatro Nacional and walk through the **Plaza de la Cultura** (Culture Square) and down the steps to the museum entrance. The museum's dazzling 2,000-piece collection of gold items made by Costa Rica's pre-Columbian inhabitants is well worth seeing.

If you feel like a rest at this point, return to the Plaza de la Cultura, head for the **Gran Hotel** and find a table on the terrace where you can relax with a drink, soak up the sunshine and watch the Central American world go by.

If it is a weekday you can explore the **Museo de Jade** (Jade Museum; Mon–Fri 8.30am–3.30pm; admission charge), just a short stroll away on the 11th floor of the National Insurance Institute (Avenida 7, Calles 9–11), which is home to the world's largest American jade collection, most of which dates from pre-Columbian times. There are great views of the city from up here.

At this stage you might want to take a taxi back to your hotel, in which case make sure that it has a meter *(maría)*, and that the driver uses it. Alternatively, if you still have plenty of energy to burn and it's not too late in the day, head for the Museo de Arte Costarricense (Museum of Costa Rican Art), which is a 10-minute taxi ride from the Gran Hotel. Or you might opt for a walk in La Sabana Park, next to the museum.

The **Museo de Arte Costarricense** (Museum of Costa Rican Art; Tues–Sat 10am–4pm, Sun 10am–2pm; free; tel: 222-7155) features a large collection of Costa Rican art from the pre-Columbian period through modern times. The museum building was once Costa Rica's airport terminal, and the surrounding park provided its runways. **La Sabana** is a large metropolitan park with tree-lined paths, a small lake, and tennis and basketball courts. It is invariably packed with *Ticos* (Costa Ricans) on Sundays and is a pleasant place to walk and people-watch. If you're thirsty, buy *una pipa* (a 'drinking coconut') from a vendor on the west side of the park. When you're ready to return to your hotel, La Sabana is a good place from which to hail a taxi. Be sure to leave the park before dusk falls, as it can be dangerous at night.

Night Options

For a taste of some typical Costa Rican fare on your first night in San José, you could try La Cocina de Leña restaurant in the El Pueblo commercial center, which is the home of numerous bars and restaurants. Another recommended option is to reserve a table at El Chicote steakhouse on the north side of La Sabana park (tel: 232-0936).

To finish off the day, check out one of the city's excellent bars or clubs, where salsa and merengue dancing are very popular. For live-entertainment listings consult *The Tico Times* or *La Nación* newspapers. Recommended nightclubs include El Cuartel de la Boca del Monte (Avenida 1, Calles 21–23), which has long been a favorite haunt of young *Ticos* and often has live music, and the Centro Comercial El Pueblo, in northeast San José, where there are clubs and bars to suit every taste.

Above: artifact at the Museo de Oro
Right: at the Plaza de la Cultura

2. HEREDIA – COFFEE COUNTRY *(see map, p26)*

An early-morning walk in the cool hills and cloud forests above the city. Join Café Britt's coffee tour, followed by lunch at a local restaurant. Visit the town of Barva, ending the day in the historic Central Plaza.

Make arrangements in advance. Hire a driver, and reserve a place on Café Britt's year-round 11am tour (tel: 260-2748; fax: 277-1699; www.coffeetour.com). There is also a 9am tour, and a 3pm tour (Dec 15–Apr 30). Take a sun-hat, umbrella and sweater, and wear walking shoes.

Heredia, one of the nation's oldest, wealthiest and most historic cities, is a bustling commercial center and the home of the National University. In the mountains, surrounded by *cafetales* (coffee plantations), the climate is cool and fresh, the landscape beautiful and green.

One of four main Central Valley cities dating from the colonial period, Heredia was founded in 1706, originally as Cubujuqui. Heredia and Cartago, the country's first capital, were conservative cities aligned with the Catholic Church and the Spanish. (San José by contrast was founded by renegade settlers banished from Cartago for defying smuggling laws; Alajuela was a free-wheeling agricultural center, where tobacco smuggling flourished.) After Costa Rica was granted independence from Spain in 1821, there was a movement in conservative Cartago and Heredia to join the Mexican Empire. The leaders of San José and Alajuela, however, wanted independent state-hood. The issue was eventually decided when armies from the assorted rival cities clashed just outside Cartago. The skirmish left 20 men dead, and the liberal forces victorious. As it happened, events to the north had already overtaken the combatants: the Mexican Empire, under the leadership of Augustine I, had fallen several days prior to the battle.

National Park

The day's itinerary begins with an early-morning walk in Hotel Chalet Tirol's cloud forest on the border of **Parque Nacional Braulio Carrillo** (Braulio Carrillo National Park). Leaving your hotel at about 8am, head north of

Above: Heredia coffee plantation

San José to pick up Highway 5, where it converges with Calle Central. Continue on Highway 5 through San Juan de Tibás and Santo Domingo, through the east side of Heredia, and up to San Rafael, where you should make a right turn uphill at the church. Follow this road for about 5km (3 miles), turn left at the fork and follow signs to Hotel Chalet Tirol. Tell the guard at the gatehouse that you are going to the hotel, then drive through a residential area and cypress forest to the hotel, where there are several well-maintained paths to follow. The one that leads to a dozen small waterfalls *(cascadas)* is particularly attractive. Afterward, you might stop at Tirol's French restaurant for a cup of coffee or hot chocolate.

Leaving Tirol by 10.30am, allow at least 30 minutes to find Café Britt: retrace your path back to San Rafael and continue down the hill to the center of Heredia, where signs point to **Café Britt's coffee tour**.

For some *comida típica* (traditional Costa Rican food) at a folksy eatery, Añoranzas (Wed–Mon; tel: 267-7406) is the place. It is on your left as you go up the hill – look out for the sign. Just up the hill, on the right, Soda La Casita also serves good *comida típica*. Another good eating place is La Casa de Doña Lela (daily 8am–9.30pm; tel: 240-2228), 2km (1 mile) beyond the Saprissa soccer stadium, on the road to Guápiles.

Back in the center of Heredia, sit on a shaded bench in the Parque Central, edged by the old city's surviving colonial-style buildings. Enjoy the passing scene in front of the impressive stone facade of the old cathedral built in 1797. At the north side of the park is a round stone defensive tower, called *el fortín*, and the **Casa de la Cultura**, with historical and art exhibits. Opposite the church, on the south side of the park, is a Pop's ice cream shop. Try one of their delicious *nieves* (fruit ices) or an *helado* (ice cream).

Colonial Barva

From the main road leading past the university, follow the signs uphill about 2km (1 mile) to **Barva**. Founded in 1561, this small colonial town (pop. 32,500) is one of the nation's oldest and most intact. Stroll around the central plaza, where the 18th-century white church and surrounding adobe-style houses have been neatly restored. Behind the church is the town's own Grotto of Lourdes, a shaded shrine to Mary. On the main street, old-fashioned dry goods stores still have their original wooden counters and *fruterias* (fresh produce stores) paint colorful, tropical still lifes with fruit.

Above: Café Britt tour bus takes a break
Right: ice cream raises smiles all round

3. TURRIALBA AND THE RIO PACUARE *(see map, p26)*

An exhilarating day of rafting. Early-morning pickup from your hotel and transportation to the banks of the Río Pacuare. Enjoy a traditional Costa Rican breakfast overlooking the Orosi Valley, and a stop on the shore of the Pacuare, returning to your hotel at dusk.

You will need to book this itinerary in advance (see below for options). Take a swimsuit and a pair of shorts, a shirt, sandals or tennis shoes that you don't mind getting wet, plus a towel and a change of clothes for the trip home. You will probably not fall into the river, but you will get wet.

Costa Rica is one of the world's great destinations for rafters. It is said that the country has more accessible whitewater rivers and rapids than anywhere else. Despite its perilous appearance, rafting is a relatively safe sport. You will receive instruction from an experienced, English-speaking river guide – who also pilots your raft – and will be fully equipped with life-jackets and helmets. The rafts, which seat six people, are accompanied by a 'safety kayaker,' who can assist if anyone should fall overboard.

Many companies run rafting trips on either the Río Reventazón (which, unfortunately, is polluted) or the Río Pacuare. All of them will arrange a pick-up from your hotel and take you to the starting point of the rafting trip, usually stopping for breakfast on the way. Among recommended companies are: Costa Rica Expeditions (tel: 257-0766; fax: 257-1665) and Ríos Tropicales (tel: 233-6455). The itinerary outlined here is run by Costa Sol (tel: 293-2150; fax: 293-2155; www.costasolrafting.com), which operates rafting trips throughout the year – rain or shine – on the Río Pacuare. Reservations should be made as far ahead as possible, although the company does try to accommodate people who arrive on the spur of the moment. Costa Sol's Pacuare rafting trip is pricey but it includes complete transportation, breakfast and lunch.

Ideal for Novices

This itinerary heads east of San José, past the whitewater capital of Turrialba, and involves rafting all the way down a 36-km (18-mile) stretch of the beautiful Pacuare River, which is well-suited to novice paddlers. There are roiling patches of white water, but also long calm expanses that are ideal for leisurely paddling and taking in a panorama of canyon, waterfalls, rolling fields of coffee, sugar cane, wild grasses and abundant birdlife. Your guide

will point out the herons, egrets, kingfishers, oropendulas and other birds that live by the river. You may be fortunate enough to see an iridescent-blue morpho butterfly, or perhaps a toucan or a sloth.

Costa Sol's minibus will pick you up at about 6.30am and take you through downtown San José to **Cartago**. Under its original name, Garcimuñoz, Cartago was established in 1561. Numerous earthquakes, floods and eruptions of nearby **Volcán Irazú** (Irazú Volcano) have destroyed much of its historical architecture, however, and little evidence remains of the colonial past. On your way through the city you will see **Las Ruinas**,

Left: look out for the elusive sloth

the ruins of a parish church that was leveled by an earthquake in 1910, as were many of its predecessors, including the original 1570 building. You will also pass Costa Rica's religious center, the grand **Basílica de Nuestra Señora de los Angeles** (Our Lady of the Angels), which was built to house a statue of a black virgin (La Negrita) that miraculously appeared on the site where the basilica now stands.

On the east side of Cartago is the settlement of **Paraíso de Cartago**, so named by Spaniards who found its cool weather and absence of malarial mosquitoes quite heavenly. From here it is a short distance to the Sanchirí Mirador and Lodge for a breakfast of fresh fruit and juice, *gallo pinto* (black beans and rice), scrambled eggs, bread and butter, and Costa Rican *café con leche* (coffee with milk). Sanchirí's dining area overlooks the Orosi Valley. Bright green coffee plants cover the hillsides, and the Río Reventazón, tamed by the Cachí hydroelectric dam upriver, flows quietly along the floor of the valley. Nearby stands La Casa del Soñador (tel: 577-1047), an enchanting wooden house carved by the late Costa Rican sculptor Macedonio Quesada and his sons.

From the Sanchirí Lodge, it is a drive of some 1¾ hours through beautiful mountain scenery, past the sugar-cane fields of Juan Viñas and the farming town and whitewater center of Turrialba, to the landing site on the Pacuare. Here you get kitted out for the rafting trip. After instruction from your guide, it is into the raft.

Hitting the Rapids

After two hours of paddling through exciting rapids and calm water, you will break for a rest on the riverbank. After a short rest, you return to the raft and continue for another two hours, past (or through) stunning waterfalls, more roiling rapids and calm, clear water. A pass through a deep river canyon marks the end of the trip. Just outside the town of Siquirres, the raft is brought ashore at a restaurant where you can change into warm, dry clothes and enjoy lunch and a cold drink before driving back to San José.

The route back to San José picks up the Caribbean Coast Highway and takes you past Guacimo, through the Braulio Carrillo National Park and over the continental divide at the highest point of the highway, just south of the Zurquí Tunnel. You should arrive back at your hotel at dusk, or just after dark.

Top: Las Ruinas are all that is left of a church repeatedly hit by earthquakes
Right: Volcán Irazú

4. OROSI VALLEY *(see map, p26)*

A day-trip to the town of Orosi, visiting Jardines Lankester (Lankester Botanical Gardens) and lunching at a former coffee *hacienda*. See the ruins of Ujarrás and the Basílica de Nuestra Señora de los Angeles.

Rent a car or book a private tour driver (see page 79). Try to leave by 8am. Take a camera, a warm sweater or jacket and an umbrella. You may need mosquito repellent at Lankester Gardens.

The Orosi Valley is simply enchanting. Fertile, dark green hills rise up from the floor of the valley where swirls of mist play with the sunlight, creating a luminous glow. Much of Costa Rica's colonial history took place in the Orosi Valley and around Cartago, and many stories of miraculous events are interwoven with historical fact.

Jardines Lankester should be visited early because it frequently rains later in the day. To get there, follow Avenida Central east through San José and the suburbs of San Pedro and Curridabat to the *autopista*. Continue through Cartago. Two blocks after the large Basílica de Nuestra Señora de los Angeles, turn right then left onto the road leading to Paraíso; you can visit the basilica on your return. Before you arrive in Paraíso you will see, on the right, a large sign with an orchid, indicating the road to Lankester Gardens.

Orchids Galore

Jardines Lankester (daily 8.30am–4.30pm; admission charge) was founded by an English botanist, Charles Lankester, who came to Costa Rica to pursue what turned out to be a failed coffee venture. Lankester bought 15 hectares (37 acres) of land to preserve local plants, especially orchids and bromeliads. Today the gardens are under the jurisdiction of the University of Costa Rica, and they feature approximately 800 species of orchid, which are best seen from February through April, when the largest number are in bloom. There are always some orchids in bloom – the gardens feature impressive displays of bromeliads, succulents, palms and bamboo.

When you are ready for a snack, and an astonishing view of the Orosi Valley, follow the road through Paraíso, turning right at the park. The road narrows and descends into the valley. Watch for signs pointing to the turnoff

for Sanchirí Lodge, a hospitable establishment run by a Costa Rican family that has owned the land for five generations *(see Itinerary 3, page 29)*. *Café con leche* is served in the traditional way, and snacks include *tortilla con queso* (a large tortilla with cheese mixed into the dough), or a bowl of *sopa pozol* (a tasty fresh corn soup).

Return to the main road and continue to the town of **Orosi**. Once you arrive on the valley floor, you will see the town's colonial church, built in 1743. Inside, there is a beautiful carved altar and oil paintings of the Stations of the Cross and the Virgin of

Left: tropical vegetation. **Above Right:** the Orosi Valley. **Right:** church ruins at Ujarrás

Guadalupe. Next door is a small museum displaying artifacts of colonial religious history.

The surrounding hills are covered with coffee plants. If it is December or January (the coffee-harvesting months) you might see coffee pickers at work. When it comes to lunch, try La Casona del Cafetal, a restaurant set in the midst of a coffee plantation (just off the road to the east of Orosi). You will see signs advertizing it on your way out of Orosi. On a sunny day, it is very pleasant to sit on the veranda of La Casona, overlooking Lake Cachí.

After lunch, continue on the road heading eastward. Soon after the Cachí dam, take the left-hand turnoff for Ujarrás. Along the way, you will see plants that resemble grapevines on stakes. These are *chayote* (a form of squash). At **Ujarrás**, which has a lovely setting, you can see the ruins of a 17th-century church dedicated to the **Virgen del Rescate de Ujarrás**, which was built to commemorate the retreat, in 1666, of a group of pirates led by the notorious Henry Morgan. The pirates had appeared to be hell-bent on sacking the country and advanced as far inland as Turrialba before suddenly and mysteriously turning tail. Some say they were tricked by the Spanish governor, Juan López de la Flor, who led them to fear an imminent ambush.

Basilica of the Dark-skinned Virgin

From Ujarrás, head back to Paraíso. If you are in need of refreshments, El Continentál, on the left just before you reach Cartago, is a good place to stop for snacks, a variety of fruit drinks and a delicious local *casado* dish of beans and rice, listed on the menu as a *plato típico*.

Cartago's impressive **Basílica de Nuestra Señora de los Angeles** (Basilica of Our Lady of the Angels) is next on the itinerary. The basilica was built to honor a statue of the dark-skinned virgin (La Negrita) that was discovered in 1635 by a young girl walking through the forest, where the basilica now stands. Whenever it was moved from the rock, the statue would miraculously keep returning there. In 1926, the basilica was built to give La Negrita a permanent home.

La Negrita is credited with performing innumerable miracles. To see the evidence, take a look inside the shrine room to the left of the basilica's altar, where there are cases packed with offerings and charms from grateful petitioners whose supplications the virgin answered. Downstairs, the walls of the basilica enclose the rock where the statue first appeared. On top of the rock is a replica of the Virgin contained in a dazzling gold case. The water from a stream running under the rock is also said to have miraculous powers, and containers of the holy water are on sale at a shed to the rear. On the other side of the street a shop sells an assortment of tiny metal charms and religious items. On the return drive, follow the Interamerican Highway from Cartago back to San José.

5. PARQUE NACIONAL VOLCAN POAS　*(see map, p26)*

Drive through mountain scenery to the Poás Volcano national park. View active volcanoes from a lookout point above the crater and follow trails through a landscape of wild flowers, mosses, bromeliads and ferns. Take lunch at a local restaurant, then visit a butterfly farm.

Make transportation arrangements as far ahead as possible. Book a rental car or a private chauffeur (see page 79). The average temperature on Poás is around 10°C (50°F), so bring a warm jacket or sweater, and pack waterproof gear. An English-Spanish dictionary would be useful.

This itinerary takes you above the city of Alajuela, high into the mountains of the Central Valley, past lots of strawberry farms, nurseries and coffee plantations, to Poás, one of the world's most accessible active volcanoes.

Try to get an early start, before 8am, if possible, because Poás becomes increasingly crowded, cloudy, misty and cold as the morning wears on. Bear in mind, too, that from May through November, there is a good chance of afternoon rain.

Take the Cañas Highway toward Alajuela. After the toll booth (75 colones), continue for about 1km (⅔ mile) to the intersection at the end of the airport runway. Turn right here, at the Hampton Inn, then immediately left, toward Alajuela. Continue on this road to Poás via San Pedro de Poás and Poasito. If you get lost, ask *¿El camino a Poás?* for directions.

On your way through **Alajuela**, you will pass the Central Park and the small but interesting **Museo Juan Santamaría** (Juan Santamaría Museum).

Above: miraculous waters at the Basilica of our Lady of the Angels

Alajuela was the birthplace of Juan Santamaría, Costa Rica's national hero. In 1856, Santamaría lost his life while setting fire to the Nicaragua head-quarters of William Walker, a notorious North American mercenary, slave trader and self-proclaimed dictator. Only in 1857, after he had invaded Guanacaste, were Walker and his men defeated by a coalition of Central American forces at the second battle of Rivas, in Nicaragua.

Bubbling Sulfur

Stay on the same road until you reach Fraijanes Lake and Chubascos. About 2km (1 mile) past Chubascos, you will connect with the road to **San Pedro de Poás**, which leads to the **Parque Nacional Volcán Poás** (admission charge). Inside the park, a footpath leads to the lookouts over a main crater that is about 1.5km (1 mile) wide and 300 meters (1,000ft) deep. The lake at the bottom of the crater changes color according to the volcanic activity at the time. If the water level is low you might see bubbling pools of molten sulfur.

Poás has erupted 20 times since 1834. The most notable of these eruptions occurred in 1888, 1904, 1905, 1910 and 1952–54. Poás has also produced toxic vapors and acid rain – one day in 1994, 400 visitors were evacuated from the park owing to vapors of sulfuric acid. Today park officials watch the emission levels and can close the park if they become unhealthy. To be on the safe side, you should spend no more than 20 minutes overlooking the crater.

Above: statue of Juan Santamaría
Right: Parque Nacional Volcán Poás crater

If you feel like undertaking a 30-minute uphill hike after viewing the active crater, head up to the lookout over Botos Lake, an ancient, inactive crater, which is now filled with rainwater. The giant-leafed plants dotted along the way are known as *sombrillas de pobre* (poor man's umbrellas).

As you come back down the path from the crater, you will find the entrance to the **Sendero de la Escalonia** (Stepping Stone Trail) not far from the picnic tables. This path leads you through an enchanting tropical wonderland of mosses, bromeliads, ferns and flowers. Your English-Spanish dictionary will help you decipher the poetry carved on signs along the trail. There is also a visitors' center with a gift shop, an interesting insect exhibit, and a café in which you can replenish your energy levels before continuing.

Guided Horseback Tour

In the unlikely event that you arrive at Poás only to find that the park has been closed owing to toxic emissions, alternative ways to spend the morning include a guided horseback ride or a hike through the countryside surrounding the park. You can rent horses from **Finca Las Lagunillas**, near the park entrance. The turnoff to the very rustic, family-run *finca* is about 2.5km

(1½ miles) below the park entrance, and from there, another 1km (⅔ mile) down a steep dirt road. Park at the sign that reads 'Lagunilla Lodge – 400 meters' and walk in. There is no phone but there are almost always horses and a guide available, and the prices are fairly reasonable.

On the way back down the road to Alajuela, you might pause at a roadside stand to buy strawberry preserves or cookies, both made by local women. Continue on to Chubascos restaurant for lunch. Sitting indoors or out, you might order *casado* (the dish of the day) and *fresas en leche* (a local drink similar to a strawberry milkshake).

After the Chubascos stop it is time to head for the **Butterfly Farm** (daily 8.30am–5pm, with tours at 8.45am, 11am, 1pm and 3pm; tel: 438-0400; fax: 438-0300; www.butterflyfarm.co.cr; admission charge). Given that this is the second-largest such farm in Latin America – some 500 different species of butterfly are raised for export here – the admission charge seems reasonable. To get there from Alajuela you should drive south toward the airport. At the traffic lights by the Shell gas station turn right, and about 300 meters/yards later take the first left, at the Ferreteria Arpe. From here it is just over 10km (6 miles) away, passing through the small settlements of Villa Bonita, El Roble and Ciruelas. At the T-junction in the center of La Guácima, turn right, go 2.5km (1½ miles) following the signposts to the Butterfly Farm. In the course of a fascinating two-hour tour you will learn all about the butterfly's life cycle. You will, of course, also get the rare opportunity to see and photograph hundreds of different species of live butterflies.

Above: one of 500 species of butterfly at Latin America's second-largest butterfly farm

The Caribbean Coast

The country's Caribbean coast is populated primarily by Creole English-speaking blacks, ethnic Chinese and indigenous people, many of whom live on reserves. Spanish is spoken, but it is a second language for many. The main centers of tourism in this region are the Tortuguero and Cahuita national parks, the village of Puerto Viejo and the stunning, palm-lined beaches of the Talamanca coast between Cahuita and the border with Panamá. Puerto Limón is a port town with a shady reputation that is worth seeing in Carnival Week (mid-Oct), when the parade involves hundreds of locals in bright costumes dancing and making music on the streets.

It is quite easy to get around the Talamanca coast by car. The Atlantic Coast Highway from San José, through the delightful scenery of the Parque Nacional Braulio Carrillo – incorporating mountains, waterfalls, canyons and virgin forest – is in reasonable condition, and the route is straightforward, if a little shrouded in mist at times. If you don't want to drive or hire a driver or car, there are comfortable express buses from San José to Puerto Limón, from where you can catch local buses to Cahuita and Puerto Viejo.

Wildlife Viewing

Tortuguero's village and park are not accessible by land, only by boat or small plane. A guided boat ride up the remote jungle canals to the park (leaving from Moín) is truly memorable. The best way to view the canals' wildlife is to arrange a trip with expert naturalist guides, such as Fran and Modesto Watson *(see page 36 for details)*, but alternative options for adventurous travelers include hitching a ride on a cargo boat or renting a dugout canoe or even a speedboat.

The park, which covers some 19,000 hectares (47,000 acres), is a haven for turtles. The name Tortuguero derives from the Spanish word *tortuga* (turtle). If you are here during the turtle breeding season (July–Sept) you may see female turtles nesting in the sand or baby turtles emerging from their nests.

On returning to Moín, you can continue your travels on the Caribbean coast or return to San José. It's a good idea to head south to Puerto Viejo, away from the crowded capital to beaches that are unsurpassed: the water is turquoise, warm and clear, and the beaches are sandy, white and palm-fringed. Puerto Viejo is renowned in surfing circles for the Salsa Brava wave that breaks over the reef from January through April.

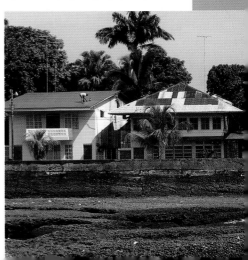

Right: homes in Puerto Limón

6. PARQUE NACIONAL TORTUGUERO *(see map, p38)*

A two-day guided tour of Tortuguero's jungle canals and the village where sea turtles nest on the beaches.

Contact the Watsons (tel/fax: 226-0986; www.tortuguerocanals.com) and make an advance reservation for the Francesca, *a canopied fiberglass boat. This tour includes transfers, boat tours, lodging and five meals. A three-day, two-night tour is also available. For this trip to the hot and humid coastal region, bring an overnight bag packed with lightweight clothing, a pair of shoes suitable for walking on wet, muddy trails, mosquito repellent, sunscreen and a protective hat.*

Situated in the country's most northeastern corner, **Parque Nacional Tortuguero** is the main nesting area in the western Caribbean for green sea turtles, which are attracted to its vast, open, windswept beaches. The park, which is not accessible by land, is reached by an extraordinary system of waterways that provide an excellent opportunity for observing the region's abundant flora and fauna. Recommended stopover options include Mawamba Lodge (www.grupomawamba.com), Pachira Lodge (www.pachiralodge.com) and Laguna Lodge (www.lagunatortuguero.com).

Modesto and Fran Watson are highly experienced guides. They know the canals intimately, and, with their trained and knowledgeable eyes, the shy inhabitants of the jungle and canals become visible: kingfishers, caimans and assorted snakes emerge from the water lilies; freshwater turtles surface on logs in the canals; howler monkeys, spider monkeys, toucans and sloths appear in the trees overhead. This is a personal tour, conducted by affable people who know and love the jungle. Fran and Modesto will pick you up in San José at 6.30am and drive you to the wharf in Moín, on the Caribbean Coast, or you can meet them at the Moín dock at 9.30am. (Secure overnight parking is available at Moín for a small fee.) Leave behind any luggage that you don't need.

Beating Deforestation

The route from San José to Moín takes you through the majestic **Parque Nacional Braulio Carrillo**, which encompasses vast, misty mountains, dense primary forests, rivers, numerous waterfalls, two extinct volcanoes and two small lakes. The park was founded in 1978 at the behest of environmentalists who feared that the construction of the highway from San José to the Caribbean coast would provide loggers with access to virgin forest, and lead to rapid deforestation of the area. You will stop for breakfast at Río Danta, a pleasant open-air restaurant in a jungle setting. From there, it is about one hour through Atlantic-slope banana plantations to Moín.

Above: on the canal to Tortuguero
Above Right: a white egret looks for food **Right:** a captive toucan makes itself heard

The river trip from Moín to Tortuguero on the *Francesca* is a leisurely three-hour ride. Keep an eye out for freshwater turtles and crocodiles basking in the canals, and for sloths, monkeys, toucans, macaws, parrots and large blue morpho butterflies in the trees. Modesto's sharp eyes are a local legend – he will ease the boat into the river bank to get a better look at the monkeys he has spotted; or he will cut the engine in a particularly beautiful spot to allow you to appreciate the silence, see the turtles' heads poking out of the water and view the egrets in the trees.

You will arrive at Tortuguero's 35-km (22-mile) stretch of beach in time for a hearty late lunch at your lodge. Then visit the **Conservation Visitors Center** outside the village of Tortuguero. The center, which is run by the Caribbean Conservation Corporation (www.cccturtle.org) is the ideal place to learn about local wildlife, and to get laminated color plates of the birds of Costa Rica.

A Timeless Village

After visiting the center, take a walk through the village of Tortuguero (pop: 600). Narrow paths wind through exuberant greenery, palm trees rustle overhead and wooden houses sit on stilts. Despite the conspicuous presence of modern restaurants, stores and *cabinas* catering to tourists, to all intents and purposes traditional village life continues in a timeless way. After dinner at the lodge at 7pm, you will probably want to devote the evening to relaxation.

If it is the right time of year, however, turtles will be nesting on the beach, in which case you could join a guided walk to see these fascinating, gigantic creatures come out of the ocean to dig their nests in the sand. The enormous tractor-tread trails that they leave in the sand as they laboriously make their way up the beaches are easily visible, even at night under a stormy sky. Green sea turtles nest from June through September, Hawksbill and Logger-heads from May through September. Each female lays 100 or more golf-

the caribbean coast

ball-size eggs in a nest that she has dug out with her flippers. In undisturbed nests, the baby turtles hatch within a couple of months. Using a temporary egg tooth, they tear open their shells and soon the entire clutch is ready to rise to the surface. A critical mass of about 100 baby turtles all pulling together is needed to excavate the sand covering them. Usually just before dawn, they emerge onto the beach and scramble for the water. But the young reptiles are vulnerable to a number of dangerous enemies, including crabs, birds, sharks and other predatory fish, as a result of which it is estimated that fewer than 0.1 percent (one in 1,000) of the baby turtles survive.

Those that do make it swim offshore to floating rafts of Sargassum weed, where they find shelter and food for their first and most difficult days at sea. For several decades green sea turtles live nomadic lives, migrating over vast distances in the open ocean. Although no one knows for certain, marine biologists estimate it takes 15–30 years for the turtles to reach sexual maturity and reconvene on the beaches where they were hatched, to carry out the next stage in their reproductive cycle.

It is a good idea to have an early night because tomorrow's wildlife-spotting trip starts early. In the course of the trip you are likely to see toucans, macaws, coatis, anteaters, otters and other animals. Return to the lodge for breakfast at 8am, and enjoy a couple of free hours, perhaps relaxing in a hammock at the lodge or on the beach.

Great Turtle Mother

Alternatively, you could take a hike to **Cerro de Tortuguero** (Tortuguero Peak), a dormant volcano not far from the mouth of the river. This spot is believed to be a sacred Mayan site that honored the Great Turtle Mother, who called female turtles to the beach to make their nests. Some locals apparently believe that an unexcavated tunnel beginning at the base of the hill leads to a chamber where the Great Turtle Mother is protected by crocodiles. Although the hike up the hill is moderately strenuous, steep and muddy, it is a worthwhile jaunt: from the top of the hill (the only high place in the area), you can see the canals winding through the jungle.

Reconvene at 9.30–10am for your return trip on the *Francesca* and a Caribbean lunch en route. The boat arrives at Moín in the early afternoon, and you will reach the Central Valley at 5–5.30pm.

7. PUERTO VIEJO *(see map, p38)*

Staying at the Villas del Caribe hotel, swim and sunbathe at Punta Uva beach, join a horseback expedition or take a guided hike into the jungle.

Pack bathing suit, sandals, tennis shoes, shorts, lightweight shirts, sunscreen, a sun hat, and a pair of long pants if you intend to ride horses. Cabina accommodations, covering the entire range from basic to luxurious, can be found opposite gorgeous stretches of white, sandy beach, edged by palm and almond trees. Villas del Caribe (tel: 750-0202; fax: 750-0203; www. villasdelcaribe.com) is particularly delightful. A moderately priced condo-style hotel, it offers two-bedroom units with fully equipped kitchens. This location is suitable for both romantic getaways and for family vacations with children. Make reservations as far ahead as possible, especially in the Christmas and Easter holidays, and over weekends in the high season.

Until the 1970s this, the Talamanca region of the coast, was populated mainly by indigenous people in the mountains, and the descendants of English-speaking immigrants from the Caribbean along the coast. It was the latter who planted the coconut trees that line the beaches, and who developed the local culinary traditions. Hemmed in by the sea on one side and mountains on the other, they did not even have roads to the rest of the country.

Surfing and Partying

Since the opening of the highway from San José, lots of new *cabinas* and hotels have sprung up, and more and more foreign visitors come to enjoy the unspoilt beaches, wonderful surfing

Above: the beaches are idyllic
Right: local transportation

the caribbean coast

opportunities and laid-back party atmosphere. Just before the turnoff for Puerto Viejo is **Hone Creek**. Hone is the name of a short palm with large roots, which bears a fruit, also called a hone, from which the locals made cooking oil. Here there is usually a checkpoint, set up in an effort to stem the flow of contraband goods from Panamá. At Hone Creek, take the road to the left.

Snorkeling and Barbecues

Puerto Viejo (Old Harbor) is a small, Caribbean town 14 km (9 miles) south of Cahuita. Many visitors to the town are surfers wanting to experience the Salsa Brava wave that breaks over the reef between January and April. In the other months of the year the sea is quiet, and good for snorkeling. To the south are some of the country's finest beaches.

As you enter Puerto Viejo you will see a rusty barge moored off the black sand beach. Continue south through the town for about 4km (2½ miles) until you reach Villas del Caribe, whose entrance is announced by a large sign on the left at Playa Chiquita. Within easy walking distance of Villas del Caribe, a few kilometers to the south, is **Punta Uva**, a quintessential Caribbean beach where crystalline, tranquil water laps quietly on palm-lined beaches of white sand. Punta Uva is particularly good for swimming. Villas del Caribe can arrange for horses, snorkeling equipment, and surf- and boogie boards. On hand are canvas beach chairs and *hibachis* (braziers) for barbecues.

If you want to take advantage of the self-catering facilities you should stock up on groceries. (Even if you don't want to cook main meals, you might want to enjoy breakfast on your balcony overlooking the

Above: the condo-style Villas del Caribe
Left: at some beaches the sand is black

beach.) Given the limited selection of groceries, especially vegetables, available in the village, it's a good idea to purchase provisions from a supermarket such as Mas por Menos before you leave the Central Valley. Don't forget to bring plenty of bottled water.

There are some fine eateries in and around Puerto Viejo, including pizzerias and sophisticated restaurants run by Italian immigrants, including A Mi Modo and La Pecora Nera. Other recommended restaurants are Soda Tamara, Lotus Gardens, Salsa Brava and Shawandha Lodge *(see restaurant listings, pages 61–4)*. If you would like to eat with a local family, ATEC *(see below)* can make recommendations. Alternatively ask around for Miss Dolly, Miss Sam or, for baked goods, Miss Daisy, who will be happy to prepare delicious meals for you so long as they have advance notice. When it comes to drinks, Restaurant Bambú is a popular place for cocktails while watching the exciting Salsa Brava waves. For entertainment later in the evening, Stanford's disco is open Thursday through Sunday nights, and Mike's Playground has DJ music every night. Be warned that, after nightfall, for all the apparent tranquility, it is inadvisable to walk alone on either the beach or on the road.

Ecotourism

In addition to swimming, surfing, boogie-boarding, cycling and horseback-riding on the beach, there are some fabulous guided tours organized through the Talamancan Ecotourism and Conservation Association (ATEC) – a grass-roots community organization. ATEC's trained English- and Spanish-speaking guides conduct a wide range of nature walks and hikes focusing on Talamanca's natural history and culture. If you want to arrange a tour with ATEC, its offices are located opposite Soda Tamara in downtown Puerto Viejo. These guided hikes are by appointment and are limited to six persons. While there, it's a good idea to buy a copy of *Coastal Talamanca: A Cultural and Ecological Guide*. (If the office is closed, check out the website at www. greencoast.com/atec.htm; tel: 750-0398; fax: 750-0191).

Another option is to ask in town for local guides. Recommended are Harry Hawkins, who specializes in medicinal herbs and Afro-Caribbean culture, and Martín Hernandez, who leads wildlife walks and ocean-diving tours.

Visitors interested in horticulture might like to spend some time at the **Finca La Isla Botanical Garden** (Fri–Mon 10am– 4pm; tel: 750-0046; admission charge) just west of Puerto Viejo at Black Beach. It was an abandoned cacao plantation that has been transformed into a working tropical plant and fruit garden. Spices, herbs and medicines are produced on the farm and you can sample homemade fruit juices.

Right: sun hat and binoculars are essential

8. MANZANILLO *(see map, p38)*

A cycle ride from Puerto Viejo to the sleepy village of Manzanillo, where you can join an excursion in a motorized dugout canoe.

Bring a bottle of water, sunscreen, sun hat, bathing suit and suitable shoes for hiking. Rent your bicycle the previous day to get an early start. There are bicycles for hire all over town or at Playa Chiquita Lodge (tel: 750-0062) about 6km (4 miles) south of Puerto Viejo.

Manzanillo is a fishing village 14km (9 miles) from Puerto Viejo at the end of the coastal road. En route from Puerto Viejo, you pass through the **Refugio Nacional de Vida Silvestre Gandoca-Manzanillo** (Gandoca and Manzanillo Wildlife Reserve), which stretches from south of Puerto Viejo to the Panamá border. The reserve covers 5,000 hectares (12,500 acres) of land and 4,500 hectares (11,000 acres) of sea and incorporates a 5-sq-km (2-sq-mile) coral reef that is rich in tropical marine life including sponges, red and black sea urchins and, occasionally, green turtles; many species of endangered animals are also protected. On dry land, most of the reserve is flat or has gently rolling hills covered with forest, grassland and farms, but hiking is limited to the coast.

Local Flavor

Willie Barton (also known as Mr Willie; tel: 759-9113), a respected community healer and fisherman, is the ideal person to take you out either on the ocean in his motorized dugout canoe, or for a medicinal-herb walk along the coastal trail. Mr Willie's house, recognizable by its veranda, is the last building at the south end of the village. When you ask him to take you out in his canoe, or for a walk, make arrangements with his wife, Miss Marva – who has established a reputation as an excellent cook – to have lunch ready for you when you get back. If walking, you might well want to stop along the way for a swim in the ocean, or for a cold drink at one of the *sodas* or *pulperías* (little grocery stores) along the way.

Central
Pacific Beaches

Costa Rica's hundreds of kilometers of Pacific coastline feature beaches and accommodations options of every description. In northern **Guanacaste Province** there are innumerable sandy stretches and resorts. Here, at the surfers' paradise of **Playa Grande**, are friendly, personal places such as Las Tortugas Hotel. Overlooking **Playa Ocotal** you will find, perched on a hill, the secluded luxury resort of El Ocotal. For nature lovers, **Lagarta Lodge** in Nosara offers a bird's-eye view of Ostional National Park, a prime turtle-nesting site, as well as trails through a private nature reserve. And of course there are large resort hotels, at **Playa Conchal**, **Playa Flamingo** and **Playa Tambor**.

To the south of the region are quiet beaches that are perfect for surfers and swimmers. Of these, **Manuel Antonio** makes for a particularly good beach holiday. Its sands are outstandingly beautiful, and it is close to the jungle and the town of Quepos, with its nightlife, restaurants and shops. Unlike many of the country's beach resorts, Manuel Antonio is accessible by car, bus or plane. From the Central Valley, the journey takes over three hours by car, about four hours by bus, and 20 minutes by plane. If sunbathing on sparkling white-sand beaches, body surfing, ocean kayaking, horseback riding and hiking in the jungle (with some live music and dancing at night) are on your agenda, Manuel Antonio is the perfect destination.

Scenic Routes

If you are driving, there are two routes to Manuel Antonio from the Central Valley, either via the highway leading through Atenas and Orotina (which is generally in good condition but can be crowded), or on the quieter, older highway to the Pacific, through Ciudad Colón, the Quítirrisi Indian Reserve and Santiago de Puriscal. Both routes are scenic and both offer interesting stops along the way. Driving time for each is approximately 3½ hours. If you want to explore the Central Pacific zone more fully before arriving at Manuel Antonio, take the old highway into the countryside and stay in a renovated farmhouse on Mastatal, a large wilderness preserve close to the old highway to the Pacific. At Mastatal, you can explore the forest, accompanied by a guide if desired, and ride horses.

If you have time to visit Quepos en route to Manuel Antonio (7km/4 miles away), you will discover the flavor of an old-time fishing and banana town. The town is burgeoning with new hotels, bars and restaurants, along with tour companies offering tours and transport to Manuel Antonio. In both towns, prior reservations are essential for all accommodations, whatever price bracket, in the holiday season.

Left: a simple local fishing technique
Right: surf's up on southern Pacific beaches

9. THE OLD HIGHWAY TO THE PACIFIC & MASTATAL
(see map below)

This beautiful route passes through unspoiled mountain terrain and a bustling agricultural center. You can visit a new national park and follow its forest trails to a waterfall and a swimming hole.

Bring hiking shoes, a sun hat, sunblock, a swimsuit and a change of clothing. Driving time to the park is approximately 2½ hours, so make an early start.

Take the highway west from San José toward Santa Ana and Ciudad Colón. About 8km (5 miles) from Ciudad Colón, the winding, uphill road passes through the **Quítirrisi Indian Reserve**, where you can purchase honey, baskets and hammocks at two colorful roadside stands. Another 5km (3 miles) along, stop in at **Antojitos K-Ceros** for a taste of *pan casero*, a sweet homemade bread and, on weekends, traditional *tamales*, corn dough filled with a mix of pork, rice, olives and carrots. If you're feeling tired, try the *Puro Carao*, a tonic made from the seeds of a jungle vine.

The bustling farming town of **Santiago de Puriscal**, the last outpost of city life before Parrita on the Pacific coast, has an impressive ruin: a grey Gothic church with two steeples, damaged by earthquakes. Follow the signs for **Parrita** along the partially paved road, which wends its way through mountains and valleys, past small farms and settlements.

Above: Puesta del Sol

central pacific beaches

To Mastatal

About 10km (6 miles) after Puriscal, in the village of **Santa Marta**, look for a huge bougainvillea tree on the left, which forms a colorful canopy over a simple *soda* (café), a good stop for breakfast or a snack. Continue 15km (9 miles) along the rather bumpy road past the village of Salitrales to the turnoff for **Mastatal**.

After 7km (4 miles) along this road you will reach Mastatal, which consists of a covered bus stop, a *soda* and **Rancho Mastatal**, an environmental learning center on a large private reserve (www.ranchomastatal.com).

A short road leads from the village to the entrance of **La Cangreja National Park** (daily 6am–2pm; admission charge). This new park has very basic facilities: a couple of concrete bathrooms and space for camping (bring your own tent). But it has a wonderful 3-km (2-mile), well-marked hiking trail through primary forest. Monkeys, toucans, parrots, coatis, armadillos and countless species of bird and butterfly frequent the area. The trail leads to a waterfall and a welcoming swimming hole with tepid water (bathing suits optional, given that this remote park has few visitors). Horses are also available in the village for rides around the countryside.

Follow the road out of Mastatal 26km (16 miles) downhill to Parrita. It's a rough road but worth the trip for the panoramic valley views and glimpses of rural life. From Parrita, it's another 25km (15 miles) to the next itinerary in Quepos and Manuel Antonio National Park.

10. PARQUE NACIONAL MANUEL ANTONIO *(see map p44)*

Hike in the national park, where wide, white sandy beaches meet the jungle. Try ocean kayaking and horseback riding in the jungle.

Book your hotel room and any necessary transportation early, especially during Easter and Christmas holidays. Bring mosquito repellent, walking shoes, plus swimsuit, sun hat, sunblock, towel, a good book, shorts, shirts and sandals for the beach, and something more dressy for a night out.

If you are not coming from Mastatal, Nature Air (tel: 220-3054) runs 20-minute flights from San José to Quepos, from where a taxi can take you to your hotel in the town of Manuel Antonio. **Manuel Antonio National Park** (Tues– Sun 7am–4pm; admission charge), which consists of 680 hectares (1,680 acres) of primary forest, swamps and tropical woodlands, is one of the country's smallest. The coastline is its true glory – three long strands of white sandy Pacific Ocean beach fringed by jungle. They are clean and wide and especially good for swimming. Above them monkeys, sloths and many other animals and birds inhabit the tall vegetation. To protect the park's eco-systems, the rangers admit a maximum of 600 people on weekdays, 800 on weekends.

Right: a Central American raccoon

You can travel between beach, town and hotel quite easily by taxi or bus, or you can rent a car. And there are lots of accommodations options – the road into the park is lined with hotels and *cabinas.*

The most striking hotel in the area is the award-winning Sí Como No (tel: 777-0777; fax 777-1093), designed to blend in with its lush surroundings. The rooms are spacious and stylish and there are freeform pools with slide and swim-up bar, plus spa and laser theater. A lower-price option is the Nature's Beachfront Aparthotel (tel: 777-1473; fax: 777-1475), one of the few places in Manuel Antonio to be built on the beach with kitchenettes and spectacular sea views.

There is plenty to do in Manuel Antonio. You might head down the road to Espadilla Beach and have an early breakfast at one of the open-air *sodas* along the beachfront just before the park entrance. When the tide is out you can walk onto the park beaches, but at high tide, when the water can be waist-high, rowboats ferry you across. At the park entrance, pay the (reasonable) admission charge and continue south to the first beach, **Espadilla del Sur**. Next is **Manuel Antonio Beach**, which provides a perfect place for a swim and has a path that leads up to scenic Cathedral Point. Beyond Manuel Antonio Beach is **Puerto Escondido**, which becomes almost completely submerged at high tide.

For a less strenuous morning, walk, drive or catch a bus down to Espadilla Beach to rent a beach umbrella and stretch out on the sand. (You can park in the shade of the trees near Mar y Sombra, but make sure that you lock the car.) Be warned that Espadilla Beach sometimes has rip tides, so if you want to swim, take the safe option and walk north a little way along the beach.

Iguana Tours (tel: 777-1262; fax: 777-2052; www.iguanatours.com) arranges river-rafting trips, coastal cruises, deep-sea fishing trips, and both ocean and mangrove kayaking. At sunset, head for El Avión, a bar with live music, a Pacific view and a real airplane. After dark, try El Gran Escape, a popular bar in Quepos with great food. For dancing, there's Arco Iris disco in Quepos or Mar y Sombra, on the beach in Manuel Antonio.

The South

the south

The southern region was one of the last areas of the country to be settled, and in many ways it remains Costa Rica's final frontier. For the first 300 years of the country's recorded history, the Talamanca Mountains seemed to present an impenetrable barrier to settlement of the southern zone. But in 1860 a mountain pass was discovered and the southern region became accessible. The opening of the road led to the colonization of the Valle de El General and the building of the Interamerican Highway, which connects San José and the Central Valley with the southern Pacific area. The south is home to proportionally more national parks and forest reserves than anywhere else in the country. It is also one of the least-visited regions.

On the way south from San José, the road ascends toward the spectacular **Cerro de la Muerte** (Mountain of Death). This, the highest mountain pass on the highway, was named after early travelers who died from either exposure to the elements or hunger while crossing the mountain. The route descends into the cool cloud forests of San Gerardo de Dota in a highland valley, where there is an excellent chance of spotting the resplendent quetzal.

Farther south is **Cerro Chirripó** (which, at 3,820 meters/12,530ft, is the country's highest mountain), the **Golfo Dulce** (with its free-port city of **Golfito**) and the magnificent **Península de Osa**. This wild, imposing peninsula features pretty sandy beaches, rocky headlands and rivers and streams that cascade over cliffs. But its biggest attraction is the **Parque Nacional Corcovado**, which is home to the country's most majestic tropical forests.

A Base for Exploration

A good way to explore the Península de Osa is from a base on the northeastern edge, at **Bahía Drake** (Drake Bay). This is said to be the place where Sir Francis Drake, the first English explorer to circumnavigate the world, landed in 1579. There are several good lodges in the area, whose staff will be happy to help with your travel arrangements; such assistance can be very useful because getting around here can present complex logistical problems.

But don't let that deter you from making the most of this region, which offers the chance of some thrilling adventures. Staying at La Paloma Lodge for instance, you can take guided hikes for wildlife-spotting in Corcovado's virgin rainforest; join a snorkeling expedition to the important pre-Columbian archeological site of Isla del Caño; paddle upriver in a kayak; or explore the jungle on horseback with an experienced local guide.

Above Left and **Left:** at Manuel Antonio
Right: proceeding at a slow pace

11. SAN GERARDO DE DOTA *(see pull-out map)*

A two-day trip to the cloud forest of San Gerardo de Dota, where you should see the hemisphere's most magnificent bird, the elusive quetzal.

Book ahead with Savegre Hotel de Montaña (tel: 740-1028; fax: 740-1027; www.savegre.co.cr). Bring hiking shoes and warm clothing, because it gets cold at night. To get there, you can rent a car, hire a driver or take the bus heading to San Isidro. The turnoff to San Gerardo de Dota is at KM80 on the Interamerican Highway, and it's a further 9km (5½ miles) along a bumpy, partially paved road to the inn. The bus stops a scenic two-hour walk away from the turnoff, though someone from the inn will pick you up for a fee.

From the Central Valley, the route passes over the spectacular Cerro de la Muerte (Mountain of Death), which rises to 3,350 meters (11,000ft). If you need a refreshment break, stop at the intersection store and *soda* at Empalme. Not far from here is the former home of the late president, José Figueres. Rain, cold and fog can make the first part of the trip somewhat unnerving, but after a while the road emerges above the clouds. Thereafter, the sunshine is usually brilliant, the air cool and crisp, and the surrounding fields of flowers and hillside farms quite picturesque. The clouds swirling through the valleys and the patches of purple foxgloves, azaleas and cala lilies are in themselves reason enough to make this trip.

Shy but Famous

The quetzal (which is officially described as 'resplendent') is Central America's most famous bird. The ancient Mayans called it the 'bird of life.' Under the impression that it would not live in captivity, they thought it symbolized freedom. And they prized its long, iridescent green tail feathers more highly than gold. The late ornithologist Alexander Skutch wrote of the quetzal: 'The pigeon-sized male owes his elegance to the

Above: the Mountain of Death
Right: the resplendent quetzal

intensity and brilliant contrasts of his colors, the sheen and glitter of his plumage, the beauty of his adornments, and the noble dignity of his posture.'

In addition to its radiant green plumage, the bird has a luminous crimson breast. Yet it is a difficult bird to spot. It lives in the cloud forests and eats *aguacatillo* – a small fruit related to the avocado. Many travelers flock to the cloud forests of Monteverde in the Central Pacific zone to spot quetzals, but they often leave disappointed. San Gerardo de Dota presents a far better chance of seeing the bird because *aguacatillos* grow here. Quetzals are most abundant and easiest to spot during their nesting season (March–May).

The Savegre Hotel de Montaña (Savegre Mountain Inn), which is run by the hospitable Chacón family, features comfortable, cozy *cabinas*, all of which have private baths. Apples, plums and peaches grow on the owner's farm and the banks of the creeks are thick with watercress. The inn does good food – the room rate includes three meals a day. Guided hikes on offer include the trail to Cerro de la Muerte, with its fabulous views of the valleys. There are less strenuous hikes through the Chacón family's mountainous estate or down San Gerardo's country roads. Anglers should appreciate the opportunity to catch trout in the Río Savegre.

12. BAHIA DRAKE *(see map, p50)*

Visit the remote, majestic Península de Osa for a trip down the Sierpe River to Bahía Drake on the Pacific.

Bring boots, insect repellent and a flashlight. See below for information on getting there and places to stay.

Situated on the northwestern coast of the **Península de Osa**, in an area of spectacular beauty, **Bahía Drake** (Drake Bay) is so inaccessible that you can get there only by boat or small plane most of the year. (There is a dirt road that's accessible during the dry season.) The rocky coastline is dotted with sandy coves and tall palms, the blue waters of the Pacific Ocean fluctuating between a deep indigo color and a luminous aquamarine as the sunlight and clouds come and go. The green hills of the jungle rise up sharply behind the beach and provide homes to squirrel monkeys, capuchin monkeys, parrots and scores of other exotic bird species.

Getting to Drake Bay

The best way to get to Drake Bay is to make reservations at one of the area's lodges and allow the lodge's staff to handle the travel arrangements. There are two ways to go: the first involves a flight to the airstrip at Palmar from San José or Quepos. From Palmar, you will travel overland through banana and palm plantations to the town of Sierpe on the calm, muddy Sierpe River, and from there, by small, open boat downriver to the Pacific.

Right: a bromeliad in the treetops

Here you will find mangroves growing along the river's edge, and lavender-colored water hyacinth thriving in the water. Watch out for the crocodiles that lurk beneath the surface. Once you arrive at the Pacific, your boatman will negotiate the incoming surf before proceeding through the waters of the ocean en route to Drake Bay. Or you can fly directly to the Drake airstrip aboard scheduled Nature Air or Sansa flights *(for details, see p78)*. On a clear day, passengers get a thrilling topographical view of the Southern Zone from the windows of the small propeller planes.

Of the numerous places to stay at Drake Bay, La Paloma Lodge (tel: 239-2801), a friendly, well-run operation built into the hillside above the bay, is a good option. You have to climb a rather steep hill to get to there, or you can get a ride on the lodge's tractor. The breezy bungalows, which are rather like elegant treehouses, extend out over the ocean. They can accommodate up to five people. Double rooms, equipped with bathrooms and decks with views, are a less expensive option.

After lunch at the lodge, head down the hill to Playa Cocolito, a picture-perfect palm-fringed beach, or swim in the pool and relax on the deck over-looking the ocean. If you would like to go on a guided sunset horseback ride on the day of your arrival, arrange it when you make your reservations.

At about 6pm guests congregate in the alfresco dining room for drinks and a discussion about their day's adventures. Dinner starts at 7pm, and conversations frequently linger long into the evening, accompanied by the sound of the surf on the beach below. At breakfast, you are likely to spot parrots and capuchin monkeys in the giant balsa tree not far from the dining area.

Wildlife-Spotting

After breakfast, you can set out on a hiking and wildlife-spotting expedition into the **Parque Nacional Corcovado** *(see Itinerary 13, below)*, or you can go snorkeling and exploring in the **Reserva Biológica Isla de Caño** (Caño Island Biological Reserve), an important archeological site 19km (12 miles) west of the lodge, a pleasant one-hour boat ride away. Caño was a pre-Columbian burial ground and its attractions include two mysterious stone spheres, which remain half-buried in the undergrowth at the highest point of the island. Thousands of spheres like these have been found in many locations in the south of Costa Rica and a few also in northern Panamá. They pose one of the country's great riddles. It is speculated that they were made in villages on the Osa Peninsula near Palmar Norte, brought to Caño in canoes, then rolled to the top of the cemetery. Smaller stone spheres, which are the size of oranges, were possibly toys but the huge spheres, over 2 meters (6ft) in diameter, may have indicated the political or social standing of the deceased.

Wildlife is scarce on the island but there are several coral reefs that offer opportunities for good snorkeling. Brilliantly colored tropical fish are easily seen by divers within 15 meters (50ft) of the shore. Between December and April 40-ton humpback whales come from their feeding grounds in Alaska, and you may spot them on your boat ride over to the island. Paloma Lodge guests are invited to fish from the boat for the evening's dinner: yellowtail tuna, dorado and wahoo are common varieties. Fishing enthusiasts can also arrange for sport fishing charters. The bill-fishing season is late January through March. Scuba-diving excursions can also be arranged.

13. Parque Nacional Corcovado   *(see map, p50)*

Take a boat trip along the Osa Peninsula's beautiful, rocky coastline and join a guided tour of the vast Corcovado National Park's virgin rainforest. A picnic lunch is followed by a hike to San Pedrillo Waterfall.

Bring good boots, water, sunscreen, a sun hat, insect repellent, swimsuit, binoculars, a camera and, during the rainy season, a poncho.

Parque Nacional Corcovado, which covers around 42,000 hectares (100,000 acres) on the remote **Península de Osa**, protects one of the earth's richest and most diverse tropical regions. This is the natural habitat of some 500 species of tree, 10,000 species of insect, hundreds of species of bird, plus frogs, lizards, turtles and many of the world's most endangered and spectacular mammals, including ocelots, pumas, jaguars and tapirs.

Prior to its establishment as a national park in 1975, the Corcovado area was inhabited by loggers, *oreros* (gold panners) and farmers given government grants to 'improve' the land. In pre-Columbian times, the Diquis Amerindians, who were known for their beautiful gold work, lived in this region. The Spanish made repeated incursions into the peninsula in search of gold; on fail-

Above: a colorful red-lored parrot
Right: the rarely spotted jaguar

ing to find the legendary Veragua mines, they plundered the natives' gold.

The mines were never located but the rumors persist. In the 1980s, when the country was suffering an economic depression, there were so many *oreros* causing such serious environmental damage that the civil guard was called in to remove them. There are still *oreros* in the park but hunters are the rangers' biggest adversary. With the advent of ecotourism, many ex-*oreros* and hunters have found new careers as rangers and guides.

This itinerary is based on a guided trip to Corcovado organized by La Paloma Lodge, which provides transportation, lunch and an English-speaking guide. Departing from the lodge at about 7am, events begin with a 30-minute boat ride in the open ocean, from Drake Bay south to the ranger station in San Pedrillo.

The hike into Corcovado from the station takes about three hours. It is not strenuous, and the pace is kept deliberately slow to optimize the opportunities for wildlife-spotting. There are steep ascents and descents, though, and the trail can be rough. Hiking boots with good traction help to prevent slips and falls, though some hikers prefer thick, rubber, calf-length boots as a protection against snake bites – which, fortunately, are rare.

Virgin Rainforest

The coastal area around San Pedrillo was deforested before it became national parkland, and the early part of the hike is through dense, 25-year-old secondary forest. Hiking inland you enter virgin (primary) rainforest, comprised of gigantic old trees with huge buttress roots covered in epiphytes and large vines. The forest floor is cool and shady. Look out for butterflies, leaf-cutter ants and their enormous nests, and fungi in many different colors. The hike heads south to the **Río Pargo**, then west to the beach. Once back at the station, the grassy area above the beach is a great spot for a picnic lunch.

The lovely sandy beach in front of the ranger station is a great place to swim, sunbathe or nap under the trees. If you have the energy, you could set off on a short hiking expedition to **San Pedrillo Falls**. The trail to the falls is quite rough, but not difficult or strenuous. On the way back you might stop for a swim in the river. Continue walking in the river – in the right direction – and you will arrive back at the station. The boat will pick you up at around 2pm, returning you to the lodge in time for a pre-prandial drink or nap – or a kayak paddle up the **Río Agujitas**.

Top: watch out for camouflaged red-eyed tree frogs when exploring the jungle
Above: the rainforest's dense vegetation conceals myriad wonders of nature

The North

The lush, verdant landscape to the north of San José rolls along the Cordillera Central (Central Mountain Range). The tropical climate here is cooler than elsewhere in the country, and the terrain is greener. This is agricultural country, with meadows and farms rather than jungles, and well-kept, relatively prosperous towns in the mountains.

Driving through the region, you are bound to notice a tidy tranquility that contrasts with the more chaotic atmosphere of the coastal regions. **Grecia**, for example, has been a candidate for the title of cleanest town in the world. You will pass lots of neat houses, in front of which stand small kiosks that sell homegrown produce, such as homemade cheese, *natilla* (sour cream), cookies and preserves. Gorgeous dahlias, roses and peach trees grow in the yards. The town of **Sarchí** is known for its carpenters, hence the many furniture and souvenir shops. **Zarcero** has an extraordinary central park filled with cypress topiary sculpted by the town's self-taught gardener.

Ring of Fire

To the north the city of **Ciudad Quesada** (also known as San Carlos owing to its proximity to the San Carlos Plains) prospers from the region's agricultural productivity. Surrounding the city you will find orchards, plantations and ranches. Northwest of San Carlos, in the **Cordillera de Guanacaste** (Guanacaste Mountains), lie seven volcanoes (Orosi, Cerro Cacao, Rincón de la Vieja, Santa María, Miravalles, Tenorio and Cerro Jilguero), some of which are active and smoking. Just south of these is the spectacular **Volcán Arenal**, one of the world's most active volcanoes, and the destination for Itinerary 14. When Arenal vents its anger, red-hot lava and huge boulders cascade down its slopes.

In the area around Arenal you can explore hot springs, waterfalls, caves and the beautiful **Laguna de Arenal** (Lake Arenal), in which the image of the quintessentially cone-shaped volcano is reflected. The lake attracts fishermen hoping to catch *guapote* (a rather spectacular-looking freshwater fish). Its western end has in recent years become an important destination for windsurfers from all over the world.

Located in the country's far north, close to the border town of Los Chiles, are the **Río Frío** (Cold River) and **Refugio Nacional de Vida Silvestre Caño Negro** (Black Cane Wildlife Refuge), which is one of the most biodiverse areas in the country. Itinerary 15 is a birding and wildlife-watching tour of this wildlife-rich region.

Right: fishing in Laguna de Arenal

14. VOLCAN ARENAL *(see map below)*

Drive through the lush northern zone to see one of the world's most active volcanoes, and have a soak in Tabacón's therapeutic waters.

The Arenal area is relatively warm, but bring a sweater for the evenings and a swimsuit if you want to sample the hot springs.

Until 1968, **Volcán Arenal** was an unremarkable, heavily wooded, low hill near the village of La Fortuna. Then one morning locals began to feel slight earth tremors. Over a period of a few weeks, the forest smoked and steamed, and women washing clothes in the creeks marveled at the increasingly warm water. Then, on July 29, Arenal exploded. The shock waves were recorded thousands of kilometers away and some 5 sq km (2 sq miles) of land was transformed from pastoral farmland to a torturous, otherwordly landscape.

Since then, Arenal has remained continuously active. It is the quintessential volcano: conical, rising sharply out of flatland vegetation, its image reflected in the waters of **Laguna de Arenal** (Lake Arenal). Nights are especially good for volcano viewing – the red-hot lava and boulders pouring from the cone stand out in dramatic relief against the dark sky. Even if Arenal happens to be shrouded in clouds, the roar and rumble of boulders tumbling down its slopes on an otherwise balmy and silent night is truly memorable.

Volcano Views

Set high on a ridge facing Arenal, the **Arenal Observatory Lodge** (tel: 692-2070) offers stunning views of the erupting volcano. Many of the rooms are designed in such a way that you can see the volcano from your bed. Prices range from expensive to very expensive and include substantial breakfasts and dinners in the lodge's dining room. For less expensive but pleasant *cabinas* with volcano views, try Hotel Los Lagos (tel: 479-8000). It is easy to reach the cabins by car. Rent a vehicle and drive through Grecia, Sarchí, Naranjo and Ciudad Quesada (San Carlos). If you don't stop, the trip takes three to four hours. A good alternative is to call Carlos Mora (tel: 232-9870 or 384-4576; email: carduma@racsa.co.cr) and arrange for him to take you. Carlos is familiar with the back roads and secret places: the waterfalls, the *sodas* with the best food, the trees where the sloths live and the places where monkeys can sometimes be seen.

Either way, from San Carlos take the route through **Bajos del Toro** (Lowlands of the Toro River) with a stop for lunch at the Asociacíon Laboral de Mujeres Bajos del Toro, a cooperative of local women. The cornbread *(pan de elote)* is particularly recommended.

Continue through the pleasant, tourist-oriented village of La Fortuna (also known as Fortuna de San Carlos) on the road to **Tabacón Hot Springs and Resort** (daily 7.30am–10pm for guests,

Above Right: therapeutic waters at Tabacón
Right: an Arenal sunset

10am–10pm for non-guests; tel: 256-1500). This is the place for a relaxing soak in pools of every description and temperature, set in the midst of beautifully landscaped grounds. Massages and facial mud masks are available and there is a good restaurant and snack bar. You might decide to stay into the evening to watch the fireworks of the erupting volcano from the pools. The weather here is mercurial: clouds enshroud Arenal as quickly as they move away. Keep your fingers crossed for a clear night.

Leave Tabacón at about 7pm and head for your choice of accommodations for dinner. If you are staying at the Observatory Lodge head west for about 4km (2½ miles) along the main highway, then turn left for 9km (6 miles) up a bumpy, gravel-and-dirt road.

There should be plenty of time in the morning for exploring the area. There is a small charge for day use of the observatory lodge's grounds, excluding use of the pool. The facilities include observation decks and rooms, and a museum complete with a seismograph that records the level of volcanic activity. You might also want to take advantage of the guided walks, which feature fantastic bird-watching opportunities and paths that lead to outstanding natural attractions such as lava flows, a waterfall and the Cerro Chata (dormant) volcano.

Dawn Balloon Flight

If you want to spend another day here, drive west along the lake shore to the village of Nuevo Arenal, for a visit to the **Jardín Botánico Arenal** (Arenal Botanical Gardens; daily Nov–May 9am–5pm, closed Sun May–Nov). Late in the afternoon is the optimum time to see the gardens, which were created by Michael Le May, an amateur horticulturist. Another exciting option is hot-air ballooning over the San Carlos Valley. Contact Costa Rica's ballooning specialist, Serendipity Adventures (tel: 558-1000; fax: 558-1010; www.serendipityadventures.com), which offers a trip into the sky just as the day is dawning and the countryside around Ciudad Quesada is waking.

15. REFUGIO NACIONAL CAÑO NEGRO *(see map, p54)*

A four-hour floating safari on the Río Frío near Caño Negro Wildlife Refuge through tropical rainforest, pastures and marshlands. Observe abundant bird and animal life in one of Costa Rica's most rural areas.

Wear lightweight clothing and bring mosquito repellent, a small bottle of drinking water, sun hat and binoculars.

You can arrange an excursion to Caño Negro through either the Arenal Observatory Lodge *(see page 54)* or through Arenal Adventures (tel: 479-9133) – one of the major tour companies in La Fortuna. This itinerary is based on an Arenal Adventures safari, which includes an English-speaking guide, transportation and lunch aboard the river boat in the price of the ticket.

Have an early breakfast, after which Arenal Adventures will pick you up from your lodge at about 7.30am. In the course of a drive of about 1½ hours, you will head north to Los Chiles, which is 3km (2 miles) from the border with Nicaragua. This is a rich agricultural area and on the way you will

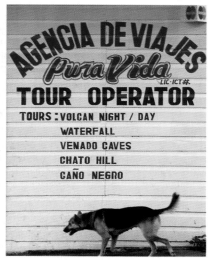

pass plantations and farms growing carob, cassava, plantain, oranges, sugar cane, papaya, beans and rice – all mainstays of the traditional Costa Rican diet. You may see armed soldiers at the roadsides; these rural guards are on the look-out for illegal migrants who have crossed the border at Los Chiles. According to some estimates there are more than half a million Nicaraguans living illegally in Costa Rica; their growing numbers pose considerable social and economic problems.

Along the Cold River

The covered-boat safari along the **Río Frío** (Cold River) commences at **Los Chiles**. You will probably see people fishing from the dock – the river is full of tarpon, snook, white drum, gar and numerous other species. Some adult tarpon are said to weigh in at over 45kg (100lbs).

Refugio Nacional de Vida Silvestre Caño Negro (Caño Negro Wildlife Refuge) is one of Costa Rica's most elusive wildlife refuges. It covers approximately 10,000 hectares (25,000 acres), including **Laguna Caño Negro**, which expands to 800 hectares (nearly 2,000 acres) in the wet season, but almost disappears during the dry season. On your four-hour river trip, which skirts the parkland north of the lake, you will pass through a diversity of habitats, including tropical rainforest, pasture and marshlands. Along the way, you are likely to see a good range of wildlife: caimans, turtles, monkeys, iguanas, sloths and lots of birds – including roseate spoonbills (sometimes mistaken for flamingoes) and jabirú, the largest bird of the region. In all, some 315 animal species have been identified here.

Above: announcing the destinations of one of La Fortuna's tour companies
Right: a typically colorful Costa Rican design from the town of Sarchí

Leisure Activities

SHOPPING

Costa Rica is not a great destination for consumers. Imported goods and clothing are heavily taxed, limited in selection and sometimes startlingly expensive. Shopping in downtown San José can be an unpleasant ordeal, compounded by crowds, traffic and noise. For attractive gifts and souvenirs try the galleries, souvenir and gift shops in the Central Valley, and at artisans' stands in downtown San José.

In recent years **shopping malls**, often anchored by large supermarkets, have sprung up in the Central Valley. The stores, which cater to the affluent, sell imported clothing and shoes, domestic items, Spanish-language books, stationery items and leather goods. The three-story **Mall San Pedro** (east of downtown San José, in San Pedro) has more than 200 stores, movie theaters and a food court. Equally impressive is the **Multiplaza** mall just off the freeway on the route to Santa Ana, opposite the El Camino Real Hotel. **Terra Mall**, in Tres Ríos, southeast of San José, is the Central Valley's newest mega mall.

Costa Ricans tend not to bargain, so there is little scope for haggling. You can try to get a discount but in most stores prices are fixed.

Environmentally conscious travelers should avoid buying coral, items made from tortoiseshell, furs or tropical hardwoods. The following list gives a few ideas of some typical Costan Rican things to buy.

Coffee

Costa Rican coffee is excellent and relatively inexpensive. Café Britt, recognized as one of the best brands of coffee in the world, is available in supermarkets and gift shops in vacuum-packed bags. *Licor de Café Britt* is a coffee liqueur comparable – but superior – to Kahlua, which comes attractively packaged in a colorful gift box. Look, too, for specialty shade-grown and organic coffee for sale in gift shops around the country.

Cigars

Fine cigars made in Cuba, Costa Rica, Nicaragua and Honduras are sold at Central Valley tobacco shops. To ensure freshness, buy from specialists rather than souvenir shops. Be wary of counterfeit Cuban cigars, and remember that it is illegal to take goods made in Cuba into the US.

Comestibles

Gift shops and supermarkets sell a variety of delicious salsa (try a Típica brand) and preserves. The most traditional local sauce, Salsa Lizano, is often eaten with *gallo pinto (see Eating Out page 61).*

Fine Arts

Costa Rica is known for its fine arts, if not its folk crafts. The work of Costa Rican sculptors and painters is shown in many local galleries. See the What's Doing section of *The Tico Times* for details of current exhibitions. In San José, Galería Namu (Avenida 7, Calles 5 & 7, tel: 256-3412) sells high-quality, authentic indigenous art and crafts.

Handmade Crafts

Woven bags and baskets dyed by Bribrí Amerindians are sold at Galería Namu, and at other stores downtown. Carved balsawood masks and gourds made by Boruca Amerindians are also widely sold. Handmade earrings and jewelry are inexpensive

Left: roadside vendor
Right: ceramics make good souvenirs

WHERE TO SHOP

San José
Galería Namu
Avenida 7, Calles 5 & 7
Tel: 256-3412
High-quality, authenticated indigenous arts and crafts.

National Association of Independent Artisans
Calle 5, Avenida 4, Plaza de la Democracia
(just outside the National Museum)
Outside sales booths featuring interesting work by independent artisans, along with cheap souvenirs.

Boutique Annemarie
Hotel Don Carlos, Calle 9, Avenida 9
Tel: 221-6707
Excellent, wide selection of Costa Rica's best souvenirs and crafts.

Pavas
Plaza Esmeralda (near US Embassy)
Tel: 296-0312
Workshops featuring artisans and gemstone-polishing; crafts and art produced by 150 or so local artists.

Moravia
Souvenir shops and arts-and-crafts galleries line two blocks in the town center not far from the Red Cross (Cruz Roja). Items from the whole region of Central and South America, including textiles from Guatemala, woolen goods from the Andes, cigars from Nicaragua and a wide assortment of other authentic items.

at the artisans' market in San José. Hand-made papers and books made from recycled bananas, coffee, wood – even mangos – and dyed with natural substances are available in many gift stores.

Leather Goods
Leather bags, wallets and briefcases are good buys in Costa Rica. There are fine leather stores in downtown San José and also in the newer shopping malls. Costa Rican shoes are generally inexpensive and well-made. Shoe stores abound in downtown San José but most feature cheap imported shoes. More expensive imported shoes are mostly found in the malls. For authentic, Costa Rican-made cowboy boots, try one of the many boot stores in Barrio México.

Wooden Items
Bowls, plates, cutting boards, boxes and the like are widely available from gift shops throughout the country. The mountain village of Sarchí is known for its woodwork, and the variety of wooden goods available in its many stores is impressive: here you will find everything from small wooden trinkets to hardwood rocking chairs, all packaged and ready to ship home. The prices in Sarchí are generally no lower than anywhere else, but the selection is large and the drive through the mountains to get there is lovely.

Finer, better-crafted wooden pieces, including handsome cigar humidors, are made by Barry Biesanz of Biesanz Wood-works (tel: 289-4337; for directions and a map, see www.biesanz.com). The crafts-man welcomes visitors to his light-filled studio and herb garden in Bello Horizonte, near Escazú.

Above: fresh from the kiln
Right: carving a wooden figure

EATING OUT

Costa Ricans traditionally start the day with a steaming glass of *café con leche* (coffee with milk) and a hearty plate of *gallo pinto con huevo*. This traditional dish comprises black beans and fried rice seasoned with onions, sweet red peppers and fresh *cilantro* (coriander leaf), with a fried egg on the side. *Gallo pinto* (literally, painted rooster) or *pinto*, is a revered national institution that seems somehow to taste best when eaten in small *sodas*.

It is customary for many Costa Ricans to go home for lunch, which is the major meal of the day. For working people who eat out, lunch usually consists of rice, black beans, cooked vegetables, a salad made with fresh cabbage, and a choice of chicken, meat or eggs, all served together on one plate. This distinctive, tasty dish is known as *casado* – 'the married man's plate.'

The wonderful quality of the local fruit constitutes one of the great pleasures of eating in Costa Rica. *Ticos* tend to be very fond of fruit and wherever you go you will see street vendors selling whatever happens to be in season at the time: papayas, pineapples, mangoes, avocados, *zapotes* (a sweet, soft local fruit) and *pejibayes* (also sometimes known as peach palms or peach nuts), to name just a few.

The majority of restaurants and cafes offer a variety of delicious drinks made from fresh fruit. These are called *naturales* or *frescos*. Among the tastiest are *maracuyá, cas* and *guanabana*. Bottled versions labeled 'Tropical' are available all over the country, but the homemade versions are still the best. Try a *mora en leche* (blackberries blended with milk, with a small quantity of ice and sugar added) or a creamy *papaya en leche* (papaya blended with milk). You might also want to sample the fresh ice creams at Pop's ice-cream stores.

In addition to establishments that serve traditional Costa Rican meals, the Central Valley has excellent international restaurants. Many restaurants throughout the country are closed on Mondays, so always call ahead to check. All restaurants charge 13 percent sales tax and 10 percent service charge on top of the advertized price.

In the following recommendations, the prices indicated are the average cost of a meal for two:

$$$ = $50 plus, including wine
$$ = $25–$50, including wine
$ = $20, excluding wine

Central Valley
San José
Bakea
Barrio Amón (near Parque Morazán)
Tel: 221-0303
Nouvelle Mediterranean cuisine with delightful Tico touches. In an elegant, arty atmosphere, the food is also presented as art. Save room for exquisite desserts. $$–$$$

Above: breakfast with a view

Café Mundo
Barrio Amón, Calle 15, Avenida 9–11
Tel: 222-6190
A restaurant in a charming old mansion that has a great atmosphere and a selection of international dishes, pizza and pasta. **$$–$$$**

El Chicote
North Sabana, Avenida Las Américas
Tel: 232-0936
Wonderful steaks, seafood and international dishes in a traditional steakhouse. **$$–$$$**

El Grano de Oro Restaurant
Hotel Grano de Oro, Calle 30, Avenida 2–4
Tel: 255-3322
Dine on sophisticated cuisine in a pretty tropical garden café or vintage dining room in San José's most elegant boutique hotel. Service is impeccable and desserts – especially the Grano de Oro cappuccino pie – are worth a visit. **$$**

Fuji
Corobicí Hotel (northeast corner of La Sabana)
Tel: 232-8122, ext: 191
This Japanese restaurant specializes in sushi, and has Eastern decor. You can have your meal in of the Tatami-covered private dining rooms. **$$$**

La Cocina de Leña
Centro Comercial El Pueblo
Tel: 255-1360
'The Wood Stove Kitchen' is situated in the popular entertainment and dining complex of El Pueblo and is one of the best-known restaurants for typical Costa Rican fare, including black bean soup, *gallo pinto*, *tamales* and beef *casado*. The rustic atmosphere is complemented by frequent folk shows and music in high season. **$$$**

La Princesa Marina
West Sabana (150 meters/yds south of Canal 7)
Tel: 232-0481
No-frills seafood at reasonable prices. Also branches in Moravia, Curridibat and Alajuela. **$$**

Little Seoul
Rohrmoser (50 meters/yds north of Plaza Mayor)
Tel: 232-5551
Japanese and Korean restaurant specializing in sushi, Korean barbecues and *teppanyaki*. **$$**

Los Antonjitos
Pavas (across from Cemaco)
Tel: 232-2411
A chain of Mexican-*Tico* restaurants found in several popular locations in San José and Escazú. Open daily; mariachi bands on Friday and Saturday. **$$**

Lubnan
Paseo Colón, Calles 22–24
Tel: 257-6071
Lebanese cuisine and classic Middle Eastern dishes. The decor has an exotic, Levantine feel. **$$**

Machu Picchu
Paseo Colón, Calle 32, Avenida 1–3
Tel: 222-7384; Fax: 225-2243
Good food at a Peruvian restaurant that has a casual, boisterous, ambience. On a night out, try a Pisco Sour and book a driver to get you home. **$$**

Nuestra Tierra
Downtown, across from the National Museum
Tel: 258-6500
Comida típica served in rustic, open-air, informal restaurant. Open 24 hours. **$–$$**

Shakti
Avenida 8, Calle 13
Tel: 222-4475
Attractive, sunny corner restaurant with

Above: popular *comida típica* fare

imaginative vegetarian cuisine and friendly service. **$**

Soda Tapia
La Sabana Park (near the Gimnasio)
Tel: 222-6734
Gallo pinto, delicious sandwiches and fruit drinks. Indoor tables and noisy patio. **$**

Teatro Nacional Café
Downtown, in the National Theater
Tel: 225-2562
An elegant yet casual place to come for lunch, dessert or just a snack, complete with great espresso and cappuccino. Marble tables, ceiling frescos and art shows. An oasis of quiet in downtown San José. **$**

Tin Jo
Calle 11, Avenida 6–8
Tel: 221-7605
The best downtown Asian restaurant does a selection of Thai, Chinese, Japanese and Indian dishes. Elegant and cozy atmosphere in a former private residence decorated with Asian themes. **$$–$$$**

Heredia
Hotel Chalet Tirol
Tel: 267-6222
Email: info@chalet-tirol.com
www.chalet-tirol.com
Lovely French restaurant in rural setting. Beautiful walks near the hotel. Call ahead for directions. **$$$**

Escazú/Santa Ana and San Antonio de Belén
Chango
Escazú (600 meters/yds south of El Cruce)
Tel: 228-1173
International cuisine, steaks, ribs and seafood. Choose a table indoors or outside on the covered veranda; big-screen TV for sports events. **$$**

Inka Grill
Paco Center, Escazú
Tel: 289-5117
Excellent Peruvian food served with flair. The seafood platters are spectacular, and the *sospira limeña* (Lima sigh) dessert is heavenly. **$$–$$$**

La Cascada
Escazú (600 meters/yds west of Los Anonos bridge)
Tel: 228-0906
Seafood and grilled steaks. One of the best steakhouses in town. **$$**

Le Monastère
Escazú (1.5km/1 mile south of Paco Center)
Tel: 289-4404
This former chapel specializes in classic French cuisine plus interesting local dishes. There are wonderful views of the illuminated city below. Reservations recommended. Less expensive pizza bar in popular basement café. **$$$**

Rancho del Macho
Santa Ana
Tel: 282-9295
Situated in the hills above Santa Ana, you can dine on a porch overlooking the city's lights. Specialties are barbecued chicken and beef. Laid-back atmosphere. Musicians on some nights. **$**

Rosti Pollo
San Rafael de Escazú and many branches
Nicaraguan-style chicken and *Tres Leches* cake. Casual ambiance. Eat at a picnic table, or take your meal home. Fast service. **$**

Taj Mahal
Escazú (1km/⅔ mile west of Paco Center)
Tel: 228-0980
The only Indian restaurant in town and worth a visit. Savor *tikka* chicken and curries in a tropical garden. **$$–$$$**

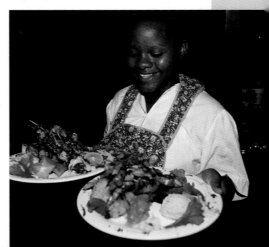

Right: Garden Restaurant, Puerto Viejo

Poás Volcano

Chubascos Restaurant
Fraijanes
Tel: 482-2069
Local fare and tasty *refrescos* (fruit juices) served in a garden on the volcano slopes. $$

Restaurant Colbert
Varablanca (1km/⅓ mile east of Poás Volcano Lodge)
Tel: 482-2776
Authentic French-country cuisine in a charming stone inn with wood stove. Breakfast, lunch and dinner are served; freshly baked croissants, baguettes and pastries available to go. $–$$

Central Pacific Beaches

La Fiesta del Maíz
La Garita de Alajuela (en route from San José to the Central Pacific beaches)
Tel: 485-5757
Wide selection of dishes made from maize (corn). Popular Tico family place, with marimba music. Open Fri–Sun and holidays only. $

Puerto Viejo

La Pecora Nera
Playa Cocles (south of Puerto Viejo)
Tel: 750-0490
World-class Italian restaurant in romantic rancho setting. Trust the chef's specials. $$$

Soda Tamara
Main Street, Puerto Viejo
Tel: 750-0148

Most reliable place in town for excellent whole fried fish and traditional coconut rice. $

Manuel Antonio/Quepos

Café Milagro
Manuel Antonio and downtown Quepos
Tel: 777-0794
Homemade baked goods, freshly roasted coffee, great breakfasts and interesting sandwiches. Newspapers and gift shop. $

El Barba Roja
Manuel Antonio (between Quepos and park entrance)
Tel: 777-0331
Authentic food in an attractive setting. $$$

El Patio Bistro Latino
Quepos (beside Milagro Coffee Roasters)
Casual breakfast and lunch menu, same as Milagro Café; sophisticated dinner menu in fairy-lit garden. $–$$

Jiuberths
Quepos (at the entrance to town)
Tel: 777-1292
Outstanding seafood, Tico-style. $$

Restaurant Bijagual
Manuel Antonio (across from Amigos del Río)
Tel: 777-4949
Generous portions of tasty *Tico*-style seafood, including fresh marlin ceviche; delicious homemade *naturales* (fresh fruit drinks). $–$$

Rico Tico Bar & Grill
Sí Como No Hotel, Manuel Antonio Park
Tel: 777-0777
Good North American and local dishes. $$$

Sunspot Bar & Grill
Makanda by the Sea Hotel, Quepos
Tel: 777-0442
Mediterranean cuisine plus fine selection of salads and seafood, served poolside under romantic tents. $$–$$$

Volcán Arenal

La Choza de Laurel
La Fortuna (behind the church)
Comida típica served at open-air tables. The wood-roasted chicken is a sure bet. $

Left: informal café society

NIGHTLIFE

If you want to sample the country's nightlife scene, you should head for the Central Valley region. Here you should not have any trouble finding all of the following: nightclubs at which the Latin dancing is so wild it might offend an Anglo-Saxon sensibility; sophisticated bars featuring talented jazz pianists; and political hangouts with *trova* (protest) music.

The best way to bring yourself up to date with what's happening during your visit is to check the 'What's Doing' section of the weekly *Tico Times*. You might want to make a point of seeing the bulletin board of the Teatro Nacional for upcoming events. An impressive array of national and international artists, including the Costa Rican National Symphony Orchestra, performs here. Teatro Melico Salazar, just west of the Teatro Nacional on Avenida 2, presents excellent, varied programs, including a large number of highly recommended dance performances.

Don't forget, if you are out in San José after dark, that for safety reasons you should use taxis rather than walk.

Listed on the following pages are some recommended venues for a good night out.

Bars

Costa Rican bars sometimes serve free *bocas* (snacks) with your drink.

San José
Café Loft
Avenida 11, Calle 3
Tel: 221-2302
New York-style chic bar downtown near Barrio Amón.

Castro's
Barrio México, Avenida 13, Calle 22
Tel: 256-8789
Open every night of the week; attracts an after-work crowd for Latin music and dancing with DJs. Crowded but fun. Take a taxi home if you're in the neighborhood in the early hours.

Chelles
Avenida Central, Calle 9
Tel: 221-1369
Old-fashioned, dimly lit *Tico* bar; great for local color and cheap beer. Open 24 hours.

Jazz Café
San Pedro
Tel: 253-8933
Best venue to hear Costa Rica's serious jazz groups, including Grammy-winning ensemble, Editus.

La Villa
San Pedro (near the university)
Tel: 280-9541
Latin *trova* music; quieter here than many places so it's easier to talk.

Above: boogie night in San José

Heredia
La Puerta de Alcalá
Tel: 267-7277
Lively and very popular. Salsa, rock and Cuban *trova* (protest) music performed by local groups.

Escazú
Big Dog's Sports Bar
Los Anonos, Escazú
Tel: 288-1872
Popular sports bar with draft on tap.

Balcony Jazz Club & Café
Just west of Plaza Colonial, Escazú
Tel: 228-8802
Jazz, soul and Caribbean beats at this sophisticated upstairs alfresco lounge with excellent food as well.

Taos
Trejos Montealegre Shopping Center
Tel: 228-6740
Two-level pub with dancing area.

Casinos
Most of the country's larger hotels have casinos. Many 'casinos' are mechanical, with noisy slot machines. Non-hotel casinos are serious, with professional dealers and professional 'working girls' on the prowl. Be careful leaving these establishments at night, especially if you are a winner.

Concerts
Check the What's Doing section in *The Tico Times* for a complete listing of concerts and

musical events throughout the Central Valley.

The Teatro Nacional hosts national and international artists, and offers concerts by the National Symphony (Apr–Nov).

Gay/Lesbian Spots
San José
La Avispa
Calle 1, Avenidas 8–10
Tel: 223-5343
Lesbian bar, but men welcome, too. Salsa and merengue. Three dance floors, pool tables, and a big-screen TV. Women only last Wed of each month.

Déjá Vu
Calle 2, Avenidas 14–16
Tel: 223-3758
This is predominantly male, but women are also welcome. Offers cabaret, pop music, and dancing.

El Bochinche
Calle 11, Avenida 10–12
Tel: 221-0500
Pop music place for predominantly gay crowd.

Movies
The following large, modern cinema complexes in the Central Valley area have excellent projection and sound systems. You can reserve seats by phone at the Plaza Mayor 1–2 in Rohrmoser, tel: 232-3271.

San Pedro Mall 1–10
San Pedro
Tel: 283-5716

Cinemark Escazú
Multiplaza, near Santa Ana
Tel: 288-1111

Left: the man with sax appeal
Above: the sign of good music

Real Mall Cariari
General Cañas Highway.

The following two, neighboring, movie theaters in San José screen non-Hollywood movies. See *The Tico Times* for subtitle details.

Sala Garbo
Avenida 2, Calle 28, San José
Tel: 222-1034

Teatro Laurence Olivier
Avenida 2, Calle 28,
San José
Tel: 222-1034

Nightclubs and Dancing

Ticos virtually always dress provocatively when they go out to dance, and the time-honored, somewhat conservative tradition of dancing with a particular partner is still observed here. Women who go to clubs alone or in all-female groups should be prepared for a lot of male attention.

The following list recommends a few old-time Costa Rican clubs where the emphasis is strictly on Latin music and dance.

San José
Centro Comerical El Pueblo
Close to Villa Turnón, northeast San José
There is something for everyone at this remarkable venue, which is a large complex of boutiques, galleries, restaurants, and bars. The highly eclectic musical offerings range from jazz and Latin fusion to Argentinian tango. Discos here include **Cocoloco**, **Ebony 56**, **Friends Disco** and the luxurious **La Plaza**.

El Cuartel de La Boca del Monte
Avenida 1, Calles 21–23
Tel: 221-0327
A popular singles bar, providing live music on weekends. Situated Downtown, near Cinema Magaly.

Barva
Tabú
North of Barva Church
Tel: 237-0521
Young dancing crowd.

Heredia
Champs
Plaza Heredia
Tel: 260-2511
Lots of university students from nearby National University. Closed Mon, Tues.

Escazú
Disco Strip
Trejos Montealegre de Escazú
An ever-changing collection of pubs and clubs attracts all age groups, and features live bands and DJs every night of the week.

Pool Halls

Pool halls in Costa Rica do not share the somewhat insalubrious reputation of their counterparts in some other countries. You'll find 'Pooles' rooms all around the country.

Theater

San José has a lively theater scene and you will usually find a play being performed in English, in addition to the various Spanish-language options.

Dance

Costa Rica's dance scene is one of the best in the world and the Central American dance esthetic is a spectacular one. The **National Dance Company** performs classical and modern works, some by Costa Rican or Central American choreographers.

The **Teatro Melico Salazar** company in San José stages productions several times a month; the company also performs at the **Teatro Nacional**. Tickets for performances are relatively inexpensive.

Traditional folk dancing is on the bill at the **Pueblo Antiguo** village in the Parque Nacional de Diversiones, an amusement park west of downtown San José.

Right: a girls' night out

SPORTS AND ACTIVITIES

Costa Rica offers some of the most varied and exciting adventure and sport activities in Central America, ranging from trekking, mountain biking, motorcycle tours, horseback riding and golf to world-class surfing, windsurfing and whitewater rafting. There are many excellent tour operators who can put together a multi-activity itinerary covering different parts of the country.

Fans of adventure sports should check out www.bungee.co.cr for information on bungee jumping, paragliding and climbing

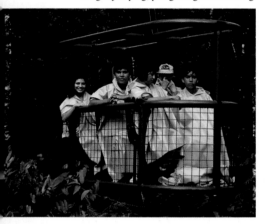

Cycling

Although the major roads are often steep and potholed and generally without shoulders, and local drivers are generally inconsiderate to cyclists, mountain biking is increasingly popular and it is possible to arrange tours lasting from a day to a week or rent a bicycle at one of the lodges and beach resorts. The area around La Fortuna and Lake Arenal is excellent with plenty of trails and good accommodations.

Bi Costa Rica
Tel/fax: 446-7585
www.yellowweb.co.cr/bicostarica.html
Bicycle tour specialists.

Coast to Coast Adventures
Tel: 280-8054
www.ctocadventures.com
Good selection of itineraries and activities.

Rock River Lodge
Arenal

Tel: 692-1180
www.rockriverlodge.com
A cozy lodge that is popular with adventure travelers. Owner Norman List is a dedicated mountain-biker and windsurfer and offers good advice, as well as renting out equipment.

Motorcycling

A few companies offer self-guided and accompanied motorcycling tours of the country. Riders need to be at least 25 and experienced:

María Alexandra Tours
Tel: 289-5552; Fax: 289-5551
www.mariaalexandratours.com
Harley-Davidson bike rentals and tours.

Moto Expedition
(bookable through Costa Rican Trails)
Tel: 225-6000; Fax: 225-8842
www.costaricanmotorcycletours.com
Offers tours throughout Costa Rica and Central America and rents KTM640s and Aprilia 650s.

Canopy Tours

There are now many ways to experience the canopy life of the rain and cloud forests of Costa Rica. They range from simple tree platforms to a ride on a modified ski-lift that takes visitors floating through the tree tops, or the more adventurous tours that entail strapping on a climbing harness and gliding along cables suspended over the canopy. There are new spin-off canopy tour companies and it is always recommended that you check out safety conditions and how the tour operates before making a reservation.

Rainforest Aerial Tram
Tel: 257-5961
www.rainforesttram.com
Only 50 minutes from San José. The most sedate way to experience the rain forest.

The Original Canopy Tour
Tel: 257-5961
www.canopytour.com
Has sites in six locations including Monteverde, where the original canopy tour was developed. The tour starts with a climb up a rope ladder through a strangler fig tree. Not recommended if you suffer from vertigo, but a unique way of experiencing and supporting the rainforest. Reservations are often necessary in the high season.

Left: all set for a canopy tour
Right: rodeo riders

Sky Walk
Monteverde
Tel: 645-5238
A tranquil option, comprising a walk along forest trails and over six suspension bridges high above the cloud forest.

Fishing
Costa Rica's marine life is an angler's dream. Along the Pacific coast anglers find some of the best blue water and inshore fishing in the world, with abundant billfish and marlin, while the canals and rivers of the northern Atlantic coast feature world-class snook and tarpon fishing. There is also good freshwater fishing in Lake Arenal and trout fishing in mountain streams. It is generally agreed that the Pacific coast is slowest from September through November while the Caribbean is slower in June and July.

A catch-and-release policy operates to protect the excellent fishing reserves, and a fishing license is required, normally organized by the guide. You can buy a fishing license at Deportes Keko, Calle 20, Avenidas 4–6 in San José (tel: 223-4142). Freshwater permits are cheap but deep-sea fishing permits are much more expensive and some visitors can pay up to $1,000 a day for world-class fishing. Good sources of information on fishing in Costa Rica are:

Carlos Barrantes, La Casa del Pescador, tackle shop at Calle 2, Avenidas 16–18, San José, tel: 222-1470.

Jerry Ruhlow, a fountain of fishing lore (tel: 282-6743, jruhlow@costaricaoutdoors.com) publishes fishing columns bimonthly in *Costa Rica Outdoors* magazine.

Golf
Golf continues to grow in popularity in Costa Rica. The best golf course is the 18-hole championship course at the **Cariari Country Club** (tel: 293-3211) and guests staying at the **Melia Cariari** (tel: 239-0022) can occasionally use the course. There is also an 18-hole course at the **Paradisus Playa Conchal Resort** in Guanacaste (tel: 654-4123) and a par-72 Ted Robinson-designed golf course at the **Marriott Los Suenos Resort** at Playa Herradura (tel: 630-9000).

Hiking
Costa Rica's national parks are ideal for trekking. Hikes can range from short nature trails in the rain forest to treks over several days, perhaps combined with mountaineering in some of the remoter areas.

Areas particularly popular with hikers include Monteverde, Rincón de la Vieja National Park, Corcovado National Park and Chirripó National Park. There is also a good selection of well-marked hiking trails in the country's growing number of private reserves.

Horseback-riding
Part of Costa Rican culture, horseback-riding is still a major part of rural life. It is easy to rent horses to explore beaches, country roads and forest trails, although a little equestrian experience is useful as *Ticos* use different saddles, stirrups and neck-rein steering. Many resort and tourist areas offer short rides or even overnight trips, but be aware that there are some unscrupulous companies that overwork their horses, especially in the

Fortuna-Monteverde area, and that the lowest-price tour is not necessarily the best.

Recommended companies include:

Brisas del Nara
Quepos
Tel: 779-1235
www.horsebacktour.com
Trips along rivers to waterfalls.

Caballeriza El Rodeo
Tel: 479-9464
www.desafiocostarica.com
Horse-friendly option for Monteverde–La Fortuna ride, booked through Desafio Adventures.

Hacienda Los Innocentes
La Cruz, Guanacaste
Tel: 679-9190; Fax: 679-9224
www.losinnocentesranch.com
Well-trained horses on large working ranch.

Lake Coter Eco-Lodge
Nuevo Arenal
Tel: 440-6768; Fax: 440-6725
www.ecolodgecostarica.com
Rides along wind-swept ridges overlooking Lake Arenal.

Scuba Diving and Snorkeling

Costa Rica's underwater wonders range from coastal reefs to offshore islands with diverse marine life such as giant manta rays, sea turtles, moray eels, white-tipped sharks, colorful coral gardens, and smaller tropical fish. Visibility depends on the season and location and is often adequate but seldom crystal-clear. The country's largest coastal reef is protected within Cahuita National Park on the Caribbean coast, where it is easy to rent snorkeling equipment and boats. There are other good places to dive between Puerto Viejo and Manzanillo, with the best visibility from March through early May and from mid-August through mid-November.

In the northwest there are dive centers at Playa del Coco, Ocotal, and Hermosa, where it is possible to learn to dive and rent equipment. Conditions are generally best from June through September.

Farther south it is possible to arrange dive trips from Drakes Bay to the reefs near Caño Island, where there are huge schools of fish, rocky corals, and undersea canyons. Experienced divers can make the 36-hour journey by sea to Cocos Island, touted by Jacques Cousteau as one of the finest deep-water dive sites in the world.

Some recommended companies include the following:

Diving Safaris
Playa Hermosa
Tel: 672-0012
www.costaricadiving.net
Possibly the best diving operation in the country. Also offers certification courses, dives, and adventure tours.

Buceo Aquatour
Punta Uva, near Puerto Viejo
Reserve dives through local hotels: El Pizote Lodge (tel: 750-0088); Hotel Punta Cocles (tel: 750-0338); or Villas del Caribe (tel: 750-0202).

variety of wilderness experiences ranging from gentle family float trips through luscious landscapes with abundant wildlife to hair-raising rides through exhilarating rapids.

Only a short drive from San José, the Reventazón is Costa Rica's best-known river, and companies *(see below)* offer a variety of day-trips and longer tours throughout the year to suit paddlers of all levels of ability.

For experienced rafters, the Pacuare is deemed to be the most challenging river, passing through lush gorges toward the Caribbean. Other popular options are the gentle Corobicí for bird-watching, the Sarapiqui and the Pascua.

The main companies specializing in whitewater rafting are:

Costa Rica Expeditions
Tel: 257-0766
www.costaricaexpeditions.com
The original rafting company, with an excellent reputation.

Ríos Tropicales
Tel: 233-6455
www.riostropicales.com
Has a variety of rafting and kayaking trips and is owned and operated by Costa Rican kayaking champions.

Aventuras Naturales
Tel: 225-3939
www.toenjoynature.com
The third main player. Runs the popular Pacuare Jungle Lodge.

Costa Sol
Tel: 293-2150; Fax: 293-2155
www.costasolrafting.com
Trips throughout the year on the Río Pacuare.

Undersea Hunter
Tel: 228-6613
www.underseahunter.com
Specializes in dive trips to Cocos Island. Sister vessel *Sea Hunter* is also available for dive-cruising. Costs approximately $3,500 for a 10-day tour from San José.

Swimming and Surfing

There is good swimming and surfing on both the Caribbean and Pacific coasts, although some beaches may not be suitable all year round. Dangers for swimmers include rip tides and large waves caused by heavy swells that may hit you unexpectedly as you leave the water. Sharks, though rare, may also be present. Always ask for advice from locals before entering the sea.

Among the best surfing beaches on the Pacific coast are: Tamarindo, Jacó, Quepos, and Dominical. On the Caribbean coast, try Puerto Viejo and Punta Uva.

For up-to-date information regarding surfing conditions, check www.surfingcr.com.

Whitewater Rafting & Kayaking

Costa Rica's mountainous topography and copious rainfall make it one of the most popular locations in the world for whitewater river running, whether you're a first-time rafter or a world-class kayaker. There is an enormous

Windsurfing

Lake Arenal is considered one of the three best places in the world to windsurf and serious windsurfers come between December and April. This period isn't recommended for beginners, as trade winds blow too strongly, but during the rest of the year, Lake Arenal is an ideal place to learn, and it is possible to arrange instruction and rental at the **Hotel Tilawa** (tel: 695-5050, www.hotel-tilawa.com). Another windsurfing – and kite surfing – center is windy Bolaños and Salinas bays, in the northwest corner of Costa Rica near the Nicaraguan border. Try the **Kite Surfing Center 2000** (tel: 672-0218).

Left: still waters on the Nicoya Peninsula
Above: back on dry land

CALENDAR OF EVENTS

Festivals, fiestas and parades in Costa Rica are often exhilarating, outrageous and sometimes even slightly alarming to visitors accustomed to more orderly and controlled public events. The huge crowds swell to unbelievable proportions, the noise rises, the excitement grows, and yet everything seems to proceed in a most peaceable way. Festivals honoring the patron saints of villages and towns are often announced by unexpected volleys of gunshots, and the loud music and festivities continue long into the night. At Costa Rican bullfights, young men simply jump into the ring to tease the bull and demonstrate their daring, while a Red Cross van stands on the sidelines in readiness. At even the largest parades, there doesn't seem to be anyone directing the traffic or restraining the crowds.

January

Festivities inaugurating the **New Year** conclude with a parade of horses and riders *(El Tope)* down Paseo Colón in downtown San José, usually on Jan 2. Central Valley horses, from humble working steeds to elegant *paso finos*, are on parade.

La **Fiesta de los Diabolitos** (Festival of the Little Devils) is an allegorical tale of the struggle between the native people (Borucas) and the Spanish. It takes place in the village of Rey Curré, in the southern zone.

The **Copa del Café** is a week-long tennis tournament in San José for the best junior players from around the world.

February

The **Monteverde Music Festival** brings together *Tico* and international musical artists to the mountain-top town for a month of concerts.

March

This is the time of year when hundreds of species of orchid blossom. Some 800 species can be seen at Lankester Gardens *(see page 30)*, some 7km (5 miles) southeast of Cartago. The **National Orchid Show** takes place in San José. For more information, write to the Orchid Association of Costa Rica, Apdo 6351, 1000 San José, Costa Rica.

The **National Symphony Season** begins at the historic Teatro Nacional in March. Performances are held in the evenings and on Sunday afternoons.

Día de Boyero, the Day of the Oxcart Driver, is celebrated in San Antonio de Escazú in mid-March. Pairs of giant oxen pulling brightly painted carts are brought to the church to be blessed.

Some 1,000 people run in **La Carrera de la Paz**, a race from the Gymnasium to the University for Peace in Ciudad Colón.

The **Bonanza Cattle Show** takes place at the Bonanza Fairgrounds, just outside the city

Above: a local amateur tries his hand at bullfighting; not an advisable pursuit for visitors limits of San José. The event includes Costa Rican-style bullfights, rodeos, and horse races.

Hundreds of artisans display their wares at the **National Handicraft Fair** held for one week in the Plaza de la Cultura in downtown San José. Consult *The Tico Times* for dates, which vary from year to year.

April

During the course of **Easter Week** *(Semana Santa)* many businesses and government offices are closed, and *Josefinos* (residents of San José) take off for vacations at the beaches and in the countryside. Any number of elaborate religious processions take pride of place in cities and villages throughout the country, including San Joaquín de Flores, San Isidro de Heredia, Santo Domingo de Heredia and Cartago.

The **International Festival of the Arts** attracts artists of all types from all over the world for 11 days of performances held at the Teatro Nacional, La Plaza de la Cultura, and at other locations.

May

Labor Day, May 1, is celebrated with workers' marches and the president's annual state address.

La Carrera de San Juan, the country's biggest annual marathon, usually attracts more than 1,000 competitors, who run the 42km (26 miles) from El Alto de Ochomongo near Cartago to San Juan de Tibás, north of San José.

July

The anniversary of the **Annexation of Guanacaste**, on July 25, is celebrated with fiestas and rodeos in Liberia and Santa Cruz in the province of Guanacaste.

This is the month when turtles start nesting on the beaches of Tortuguero.

August

On August 1 and 2, thousands of the faithful make a **pilgrimage** from San José to Cartago in honor of the country's patron saint, the **Virgen de Los Angeles**. A statue of the Black Virgin (known as La Negrita) miraculously appeared in the forest where Cartago's basilica now stands. Many miracles are attributed to the beloved Virgin, as the result of which her shrine is full of offerings from petitioners whose prayers she has answered.

The **Credomatic International Music Festival** is held in venues across the country.

September–October

September 15 is Costa Rica's **Independence Day**. Parades featuring marching bands take place throughout the country. At 6pm traffic throughout the country comes to a halt and everyone sings the national anthem.

October 12, **Columbus Day** (or El Día de las Culturas, as it is now called), is the occasion of a week-long carnival in Puerto Limón. The highlight of Carnival Week is the parade, when thousands take to the streets to join in a great spectacle of music and dance.

On the beaches of Guanacaste and Tortuguero, the turtles approach the end of their nesting season.

December

During the week between Christmas and New Year, there is a nightly **carnival** at the fairground in Zapote. It features fairground rides, special carnival food and Costa Rican-style bullfights, at which amateur and aspiring professional matadors jump into the bullring to harass the bulls. Although it is said that the bulls are never physically harmed, the young men sometimes do themselves considerable damage.

Right: supplicants at Cartago

Practical
Information

GETTING THERE

By Air
Although many international flights to Costa Rica now arrive at Daniel Oduber/Tomas Guardia Airport in Liberia (Guanacaste Province), most still land at Juan Santamaría International Airport, a 20-minute drive from San José. Cab rides to Central Valley hotels are fixed at US$13–20, depending on distance. Passengers pay at a kiosk at the airport, not the driver. The bus fare into town is very cheap.

Make reservations for your flight as far ahead as possible, especially if you plan to travel between December and February or at Easter. Ask for your confirmation number. It is best to confirm your reservation 72 hours before departure and arrive at the airport at least two hours in advance.

Airport Tax
There is an exit tax (US$26 at the time of going to press) for departing tourists. This is not usually included in the price of your ticket.

By Road
The Interamerican Highway allows for fairly rapid transit into Costa Rica. If you take a vehicle into the country, it will be noted on your passport. Leaving the country without the vehicle, once it has been noted, can be problematic. It may be necessary to show the border authorities that you have a sufficient supply of cash for your stay.

Tica Bus (tel: 221-8581; www.ticabus.com) provides a comfortable and reliable bus service throughout Central America. There is a daily bus service from Nicaragua and Panamá to Costa Rica.

By Sea
Cruise ships arrive at Puerto Limón, on the Atlantic coast, and at Puntarenas, on the Pacific. Check with a travel agent to find out which cruise lines sail to Costa Rica.

Left: slowly does it
Right: cruising Costa Rican-style

Puntarenas, on the Pacific coast, has a well-managed yacht club, which is one of the first stops for transoceanic yachts from Western USA ports of call.

TRAVEL ESSENTIALS

When to Visit
In the Central Valley, the dry season generally lasts from December through April. This is the high season, especially between Christmas and New Year, and during the Easter holiday, when it can be extremely difficult to reserve airline tickets, lodgings or rental cars.

The rainy season is between May and November, when most mornings are bright and sunny but afternoons often bring rain. The vegetation is green and fresh, and 'green season' discounts are often available at hotels. November is an ideal time to visit, when the rains are subsiding but the high season is not in full swing. On the Caribbean coast, however, rain can fall at any time.

Visas and Passports
Citizens of Canada, the UK, the USA and many European countries are given 90-day visas on entering Costa Rica. Citizens of other countries are usually given 30-day visas. Check on the latest regulations before leaving home.

Visitors must have a pre-paid airline ticket to another country in order to enter Costa Rica, although a bus ticket to a neighboring country will often suffice.

Always carry your passport with you (or, for safety, a photocopy of the identification pages and the page with your entry stamp), and report any lost ID immediately.

For further information, contact the Embassy of Costa Rica, Washington, DC 20008, or the Costa Rican Tourism Institute (Instituto Costarricense de Turismo), tel: 223-1733; toll free telephone number from the USA 1-800/343-6332; fax: 223-5452; www.visitcostarica.com.

In San José, UK citizens can contact the British Embassy at Edificio Centro Colón, 11th floor, Paseo Colón, Calles 38 and 40, tel: 258-2025, fax: 233-9938; www.embajada britanica.com. The US Embassy is situated in front of Centro Comercial on Carretera Pavas, tel: 220-3939, fax: 220-2305; www. usembassy.or.cr.

Vaccinations

No vaccinations are required in order to visit Costa Rica unless coming from a yellow fever or cholera area. Malaria is not a problem here, except in remote regions of Talamanca. Cholera is not generally a problem either, but away from hotels and restaurants it is perhaps wise to avoid ice and unpeeled fruit. There have been cases of dengue fever, which is carried by mosquitoes. Take adequate precautions to avoid being bitten, especially in lowland urban areas such as Liberia and Puerto Limón.

Customs

Travelers are usually waved through customs or given only a cursory check, unless carrying excessive baggage. A maximum of six rolls of film, 500 grams (18 oz) of tobacco, 2kg (4.4 lbs) of candy, and 3 liters (106 fl.oz) of wine or liquor (for travelers aged over 21) can be brought in to the country. Prescription drugs should be kept in original containers. Costa Rica is serious about halting the flow of illegal drugs; don't risk carrying them.

Weather

The average temperature in San José and environs is about 24°C (75°F). In the highlands, temperatures drop approximately 0.6°C (1.8°F) for each 100 meters (330ft) of elevation. Temperatures along the coasts range from the mid-20s°C (70s°F) to the 30s°C plus (low 90s°F), usually accompanied by high humidity.

Clothing

Bring clothes and shoes suitable for the activities you plan to undertake (hiking, rafting, horseback riding, etc.) as well as smarter clothes for San José restaurants and nightlife.

Costa Ricans used to dress rather more formally than most Europeans and North Americans, but casual jeans and very sexy clothes are more common now. Shorts are still mostly worn for sports and at the beach, not in cities. Sweaters and jackets are needed for cool evenings and in the mountains.

Bring raingear and shoes that are suitable for muddy trails if you plan to hike. A sunhat and umbrella are also useful, and it is a good idea to bring your accustomed brand of insect repellent, medications, sunscreen, tampons and contraceptives with you since they may be difficult to purchase outside San José. Nature lovers should remember to bring binoculars and a flashlight.

Electricity

Electricity runs at 110 volts AC, 60Hz, and sockets are made for two-prong flat and round plugs. American and Canadian appliances, whose plugs do not have grounding prongs, will usually work here.

Time Differences

GMT minus six hours, the same as Central Time in the USA. There is no daylight savings change, so it is usually dark, year-round by around 6pm.

GETTING ACQUAINTED

Geography

Costa Rica is situated near the center of the Central American isthmus, with Nicaragua to the north and Panamá to the south. To the east is the Atlantic Ocean, with beautiful Caribbean beaches, and to the west are hundreds of kilometers of Pacific coastline.

It is a small country, one of the smallest in Latin America, covering less than 52,000 sq km (20,000 sq miles). There are steamy coastal plains and beaches of every description, high mountains, unmapped virgin rainforests, cloud forests, tropical dry forests, jungles, mangrove swamps, plains and pastures and active volcanoes.

The diversity of animal life matches the diversity of landscapes: there are more than 850 species of birds; around 130 species of freshwater fish; 208 species of mammals, including big cats; approximately 1,000 species of butterflies; and hundreds of thousands of species of insects.

Government and Economy

Costa Rica is a democracy governed by a president, two vice-presidents and a legislative assembly. Elections are held every four years. The constitution, adopted in 1949 after a civil war, abolished the military. Costa Rica has one of the highest living standards in the southern hemisphere, free public health care and education, and one of the highest literacy rates (95 percent) in all the Americas.

Tourism and electronics are Costa Rica's biggest sources of foreign income, with pineapples making up a growing part of the country's agricultural economy as coffee and bananas decline in importance.

Religion

The majority of Costa Ricans are Catholic (76 percent), although Protestant Evangelical religions are becoming increasingly popular. There is a small Jewish community in San José, and a small community of Friends (Quakers) in Monteverde.

How Not to Offend

Costa Ricans tend to be quite formal, reserved and polite. Spanish speakers will be interested to note that the informal *tu* is almost never used. The formal 'you,' *usted*, is even used within the family and between good friends. It is best to stick with *usted*, which is always correct. The best way to get along in Costa Rica is to be friendly, polite and calm. Avoid raising one's voice, getting angry, or causing another to 'lose face.'

Population (Ethnicity)

Racially, the population of Costa Rica is rather complex. About 1 percent of the population are *Indígenas* or native inhabitants, who live in the more remote areas of the country, often on reserves. Costa Ricans of the Central Valley are predominantly of Spanish descent. They speak Spanish and proudly refer to themselves as *Ticos*. The people of Guanacaste, many of whom are descended from the Chorotega Amerindians, resemble their Nicaraguan neighbors in manner and accent, and call themselves *Guanacastecos*.

Black Costa Ricans *(Negros)* of the Caribbean coast region, whose ancestors were Jamaican workers who came to Costa Rica to fish or work on the Atlantic Railroad, speak English and Spanish. There are also many Chinese Costa Ricans *(Chinos),* whose forebears also came to construct the railroad.

The most recently arrived immigrant groups in Costa Rica are the Europeans and North Americans *(Gringos),* and political and economic refugees *(Nicas)* from Nicaragua.

Above: a rich ethnic mix

MONEY MATTERS

Currency
The unit of currency is the colón. Money can be changed at the airport until 5pm. US dollars are accepted in most tourist towns.

Money Changers
The service in national banks is notoriously slow, and having to wait in line for an hour to change money is not uncommon. Instead, look for ATH ('*a todas horas*' – at all hours) automatic cash machines that accept foreign bank cards allied with international systems. It is increasingly easy to find cash machines in shopping centers and offices, but beware, as there may be hidden charges.

National banks are open weekdays 9am–4.30pm; private banks open 8am–3.30pm. The current rate of exchange can be found in the daily newspaper, and the English-language *Tico Times*.

Change colones back into dollars before departing from Costa Rica. The airport bank will cash only $50 worth of colones for departing travelers.

It is advisable to buy travelers' checks and cash in small denominations. You may not be able to break 5,000 colón notes when paying for taxis and other services, so bear this in mind.

Credit Cards
American Express, Visa and MasterCard are widely accepted at restaurants and hotels in the Central Valley. But if you travel to the beaches or the mountains you will probably need cash or travelers' checks, except at large hotels. It is common for hotels and other tourist establishments to add a 7–8 percent surcharge to purchases with credit cards. Check before using your card, as this is not strictly legal.

If your card is lost or stolen you can call the following numbers:
Credomatic (for American Express and MasterCard): 295-9898.
Visa: 224-2631.

Tipping
Restaurants add a 10 percent gratuity to your check, but it's customary to leave an additional tip of perhaps 5 percent, if the service warrants it. Hotel bellboys, maids and tour guides should also be tipped.

Taxes
Hotels and restaurants add a 13 percent sales tax to your bill and 10 percent service charge. Hotels also add a 3.45 percent tourism tax on room charges.

GETTING AROUND

Domestic Flights
Domestic flights are fairly inexpensive and can provide a comfortable alternative to many hours on bad roads. Sansa and Nature Air (recommended) serve many destinations. Domestic flights fly into Juan Santamaría Airport (Sansa) or Tobias Bolaños Airport in Pavas. It is also possible to charter flights and to book helicopter tours.
Aero Costa Sol, tel: 440-1444; fax: 441-2671; www.aerocostasol.com. Charter flights.
Helicópteros Turísticos Tropical, tel: 296-0460. Helicopter tours.
Sansa, tel: 221-9414; fax: 255-2176; www.flysansa.com.
Nature Air, tel: 220-3054; fax: 220-0413; www.natureair.com.

Above: negotiating a fare
Right: flying over Central Valley

Taxis

Licensed taxis are red with a taxi sign on the roof. They are widely used and inexpensive – fares within San José are generally just a few dollars. All taxis are supposed to have working meters *(marías)*. If your driver has no *maría*, negotiate the fare before getting in, or find a taxi whose *maría* is working.

If you are greatly overcharged write down the driver's name and license number, and call the taxi company number marked on the outside of the cab.

Buses

You can travel anywhere in Costa Rica by bus. Consider taking at least one bus trip during your visit, if only to a nearby Central Valley town, as it is a good way to experience local life.

The main bus stop in the center of San José is the Coca-Cola terminal, at Calle 16, Avenidas 1–3. The Costa Rican Tourist Institute (ICT) office, below Plaza de la Cultura, has a list of bus companies' names and telephone numbers (tel: 223-1733). The weekly English- and Spanish-language newspaper, *Costa Rica Today*, often carries a page of current bus information.

Rental Cars

Rental cars are not recommended for getting around San José, but make sense for trips outside the city, though driving conditions can be quite trying. Consider using public transportation or a paid driver for your first day or two, before you decide whether you wish to take to the wheel yourself.

Car rental rates are generally around US$40–60 per day, including insurance. Four-wheel drive vehicles (recommended for many areas outside the Central Valley, especially during the rainy season) are usually around US$80 per day. Reserve your vehicle as far in advance as possible and get written confirmation. Pre-payment is advised, especially during the high season (Dec–Feb) and during the Easter vacation.

Among the better car-rental companies are: Alamo, tel: 233-7733; Dollar, tel: 257-0671; Elegante, one of the few which offers non-deductible insurance, tel: 668-1054; toll-free 1/800-582-7432 from the USA; Toyota, tel: 258-5797; and Economy, tel: 231-5410.

Driving in Costa Rica

The government has invested heavily in improving the roads over the past decade, but some are still in poor condition. Drivers weave all over the road to avoid the sometimes enormous potholes *(huecos)* and so will you, after you've hit a few. In addition, in the wet-season months of June through November, the roads can be prone to landslides and floods. Two main-beam blinks usually indicate that the other driver is allowing you the right-of-way.

If you are waved over by the police, pull over. Don't try to drive away, as they will simply radio ahead to have you stopped. Be sure to have all automobile documents in the car, and be polite.

It is illegal for police to demand on-the-spot payment of fines for traffic violation or to solicit a bribe. Wear your seatbelt and observe the speed limits (radar is often used on the highways).

Don't drive without insurance and a valid driver's license. If you are in an accident, don't move your vehicle until the police come, otherwise it will be assumed that you are the guilty party.

In the cities, park your car in one of the inexpensive, attended parking lots *(parqueos)*. Avoid parking illegally, as violators' cars are sometimes towed away. Always lock your vehicle, and never leave any valuables inside.

Private Tour Drivers

Hiring a skilled, English-speaking driver, experienced with Costa Rican roads, is a good way to become familiar with driving conditions and a much more relaxing way of getting to your destination. For information call the ICT (Costa Rican Tourism Institute), tel: 223-1733, or contact a reputable local tour operator to book a car with driver.

Ferries

Puntarenas to Playa Naranjo: departs 6am, 10.50am, 2.20pm and 7pm.
Playa Naranjo to Puntarenas: departs 7.30am, 12.30pm, 5pm and 9pm.
Puntarenas to Paquera: departs 4.30am, 8.30am, 12.30pm and 5.30pm.
Paquera to Puntarenas: departs 6.30am, 10.30am, 3pm and 8.30pm.

Schedules change constantly; always check timings in advance.

HOURS AND HOLIDAYS

Business Hours

Business hours are generally Monday to Friday 9am–5pm, with a two-hour lunch break from noon–2pm. National banks usually open 9am–4.30pm on weekdays with some staying open until 7pm in San José; private banks open from 8am and close anytime between 3.30 and 5pm, depending on the bank. Stores are generally open Mon– Sat 8am–7pm. Some shopping malls are open on Sundays and in the evenings.

Public Holidays and Festivals

January 1: New Year's Day.
Mid-January: Fiesta de Santa Cruz (Nicoya Peninsula), rodeos, bullfights, music and dancing.
March 19: Feast of St Joseph (patron saint of San José).
April 11: Anniversary of Battle of Rivas (Juan Santamaría Day).
Maundy Thursday to Easter Sunday
May 1: Labor Day.
June (Thursday after Trinity Sunday): Corpus Christi.
June (third Sunday): Father's Day.
June 29: Feasts of St Peter and St Paul.
July 25: Annexation of Guanacaste Province.

August 2: Feast of Our Lady of the Angels (patron saint of Costa Rica).
August 15: Assumption of the Blessed Virgin; also Mother's Day.
September 15: Independence Day.
October 12: Columbus Day, now called El Día de las Culturas.
Mid-October: a week-long Carnival held in Puerto Limón.
December 24–25: Christmas Eve and Christmas Day.

Government and business offices, including banks and post offices, are virtually closed down from Christmas to the New Year and in the latter part of Easter week *(Semana Santa)*. Generally, buses do not run on Good Friday, so make sure you have other means of transportation during this period. Bars are sealed Thursday to Saturday during Holy Week and there is no liquor sold from Thursday night before a Sunday election until the Monday after the election.

Market Days

Saturday morning is market day in Escazú and Heredia. A huge variety of local fruit and vegetables, as well as fresh flowers, honey and baked goods are sold.

ACCOMMODATIONS

It is advisable to book ahead if you want to stay in any of the big luxury hotels, especially during high season and at Christmas or Easter. A sales tax of 13 percent and a tourism tax of 3.39 percent are added to all accommodations bills. Price brackets, which are based on two people sharing a double room, are as follows:

$$$$	$100–300
$$$	$70–90
$$	$40–70
$	$20–40

San José/Central Valley

There is a wide choice of accommodations in downtown San José and its surrounding suburbs, ranging from budget backpackers' hostels to charming inns. Those visitors with only a short time in San José may prefer to stay downtown in one of the renovated older

Left: market day

houses, but many visitors prefer to stay in one of the suburbs such as Escazú, which is only 15 minutes west of the city and has wonderful views of the Central Valley.

Downtown

Fleur de Lys Hotel
Calle 13, Avenidas 2 & 6
Tel: 223-1206; Fax: 257-3637
www.hotelfleurdelys.com
Located close to the National Museum of San José and only five-minutes' walk from downtown, this elegantly restored mansion has 19 rooms individually decorated. **$$$**

Hotel Grano de Oro
Calle 30, Avenidas 2–4
Tel: 255-3322; Fax: 221-2782
www.hotelgranodeoro.com
Charming converted 19th-century mansion with pretty courtyards and fountains, excellent garden restaurant and 35 unique rooms and suites. Quiet location and panoramic views of the city, plus excellent service. Early booking recommended. **$$$–$$$$**

Escazú

Hotel Alta
Alto de las Palomas
Tel: 282-4160; Fax: 282-4162
www.thealtahotel.com
Well worth the expense, this gem of a hotel lies 8km (5 miles) west of San José between Escazú and Santa Ana with spectacular views over the valley and city. Infused with colonial charm, the individually designed guestrooms have custom-made furnishings and every modern convenience. Facilities include the excellent La Luz Restaurant, swimming pool and health spa. **$$$$**

Casa de las Tias
San Rafael de Escazú
Tel: 289-5517; Fax: 289-7353
www.hotels.co.cr/casatias.html
Sprawling Victorian-style house set in lush gardens. Friendly hosts; original Latin American art and private baths. **$$–$$$**

Hotel Posada el Quijote
Bello Horizonte de Escazú
Tel: 289-8401; Fax: 289-8729
www.quijote.co.cr

This is a lovely country home, converted into a B&B adorned with a modern art collection and attractive gardens and offering panoramic views. **$$$**

San Gildar
Between Escazú and Santa Ana on the old highway
Tel: 289-8843; Fax: 228-6454
www.hotelsangildar.com
A pleasant luxury/business hotel with lush tropical gardens, pool, restaurant and bar. The third-floor rooms are generally the most quiet. **$$$–$$$$**

Tara Resort Hotel & Spa
Signposted from Escazú
Tel: 228-6992; Fax: 228-9651
www.tararesort.com
A plantation-style mansion and spa that could have come straight out of *Gone With the Wind*. It offers heaps of southern grandeur and a spectacular setting overlooking the Central Valley. Wide variety of spa treatments available. **$$$$**

Heredia and Airport Area

Hotel Costa Rica Marriott
San Antonio de Belén, five minutes from the airport
Tel: 298-0000; Fax: 298-0044
www.costarica-marriott.com
Attractive colonial-style resort located in a coffee plantation with superb leisure facilities, including two swimming pools, golf, tennis and health club plus a choice of excellent dining options. A good base for a longer stay in the San José area. **$$$$**

Hotel and Spa Xandari
Alajuela
Tel: 443-2020; Fax: 442-4847
www.xandari.com
A 15-minute drive from the airport and set in a peaceful coffee plantation on a ridge overlooking the Central Valley, this is a tiny hotel of striking architectural design comprising 21 villas. Delicious breakfasts are served on a large terrace and main meals are served in the lodge. There are two swimming pools and a jacuzzi, as well as an outdoor gym. **$$$$**

Finca Rosa Blanca Country Inn
Santa Bárbara de Heredia
Tel: 269-9392; Fax: 269-9555
www.finca-rblanca.co.cr
An extraordinary small hotel in the foothills of Heredia. Romantic and fanciful with eclectic architecture and original art. $$$$

Turrialba
Casa Turire
Turrialba
Tel: 531-1111; Fax: 531-1075
www.hotelcasaturire.com
Located 90 minutes' drive from San José, the colonial-style Casa Turire is the luxurious centerpiece of a spectacular coffee, macadamia nut and sugar cane plantation on the banks of the Reventazón River at the base of the Turrialba Mountains. It has 16 elegant rooms and suites, a gourmet restaurant, spring-fed pool, jacuzzi, tennis and putting. Good base for hiking, rafting and tours to the pre-Columbian Guayabo ruins. $$$$

Parque Nacional Volcan Poás
Poás Volcano Lodge
Less than 1km (½ mile) from Varablanca
Tel/fax: 482-2194
www.poasvolcanolodge.com
This eco-lodge is set at an altitude of 1,900 meters (6,233ft), with stunning views over the northern Caribbean plains, the Atlantic coastline and Poás Volcano. Warm and spacious accommodations, lovely main sitting area with sunken fireplace, billiard room, healthy cuisine, exuberant gardens, jungle trails and many other outdoor activities, such as horseback-riding, cycling and whitewater rafting. Definitely the best lodge in the area. $$$–$$$$

The Caribbean Coast
Parque Nacional Tortuguero
If possible, visit Tortuguero either between February and July for the nesting season of the leatherback turtle or July through October for that of the green turtle. Most visitors spend at least two nights in the park, and a number of lodges provide comfortable accommodations, guides, boats and family-style dining. Most of the lodges can be booked as part of an itinerary (including transportation) through one of the many San José operators or through the lodge itself.

There are more basic places to stay in Tortuguero, costing approximately $8–20 per person but excluding meals, activities and the services of a guide.

Laguna Lodge
Tortuguero
Tel: 225-3740; Fax: 283-8031
www.lagunatortuguero.com
A small and cozy lodge on a narrow strip of land between the Caribbean Sea and the Tortuguero Lagoon, with free-form pool, rustic restaurant and hammock huts scattered throughout the 5-hectare (12-acre) 'rainforest' garden. The lodge offers 30 rooms with fans and private facilities. $$$

Mawamba Lodge
Tortuguero
Tel: 223-2421; Fax: 222-5463
www.mawamba.com
A short hike from Tortuguero town, this 6-hectare (15-acre) beachfront lodge has lush gardens with exotic birds and rustic, fan-cooled accommodations. Swimming pool with jacuzzi, two family-style restaurants, bar, souvenir shop, and access to beach (though sea swimming is not recommended anywhere around Tortuguero). Boat ride and guided forest hike included in the rates. There is the possibility of arranging fishing or night turtle hikes. $$$

Pachira Lodge
Tortuguero

Tel: 256-7080; Fax: 223-1119
www.pachiralodge.com
Located only five minutes away from Tortuguero National Park, the lodge has 42 comfortable rooms, charmingly decorated with pastels and bamboo, built on stilts and connected by covered walkways. The lodge has a bar and restaurant and three nature trails, plus all the usual tours. $$$

Pacuare Nature Reserve
30km (19 miles) northwest of Puerto Limón
Tel: 233-0508
www.rainforestconcern.org
An 800-hectare (1,976-acre) private reserve co-run by the Endangered Wildlife Trust and Rainforest Concern which is open to eco-tourists and volunteers who wish to participate in the turtle protection program. A beautiful lodge with only three bedrooms overlooks the beach and a freshwater lagoon that opens onto the main Tortuguero canal. The 6-km (3¾-mile) beach is one of the most important nesting sites for the leatherback turtle. Green turtles nest here from June through September. Price includes transportation by boat, boat tour, meals and lodging. $$$

Tortuga Lodge
Tortuguero
Tel: 257-0766; Fax: 257-1665
www.costaricaexpeditions.com
Tortuga Lodge was the first lodge in the area and has won eco-tourism awards for its support of the local community and its solar energy. There are landscaped gardens as well as easy access to the rainforest, where howler monkeys and poison-arrow frogs may be spotted. $$$$

Cahuita

B&B El Encanto
Tel/fax: 755-0113
www.elencantobedandbreakfast.com
Attractive bungalows and lodge set in peaceful Zen garden; homemade breads accompany bountiful breakfasts. $$

Puerto Viejo

El Pizote Lodge
Puerto Viejo
Tel: 750-0088; Fax: 750-0226

www.pizotelodge.com
Surrounded by the jungle of Talamanca, the lodge is a 10-minute walk west from Puerto Viejo just across from the black beach. Some of the rooms and bungalows have private facilities. Restaurant, bar and pool, plus cycles, snorkeling and riding. $$$

Selva Bananito Lodge
Between Puerto Limón and Cahuita
Tel/fax: 253-8118
www.selvabananito.com
This secluded and comfortable family-run rainforest lodge and reserve is an excellent place to watch birds, climb trees and rappel down waterfalls, take camping and riding trips or learn Spanish. $$

Shawandha Lodge
Puerto Viejo
Tel: 750-0018; Fax: 750-0037
www.shawandhalodge.com
Shawandha is designed like a primitive village nestled in more than two hectares (5 acres) of enormous ceiba trees and colorful tropical flowers. Each thatched bungalow has a romantic atmosphere, with traditional furnishings, large verandah, and unusual bathrooms. Good restaurant, and a 150-meter (490-ft) private trail leads to the white sands of Playa Chiquita. $$$$

Villas del Caribe
Playa Chiquita, near Puerto Viejo
Tel: 750-0202
www.villasdecaribe.com

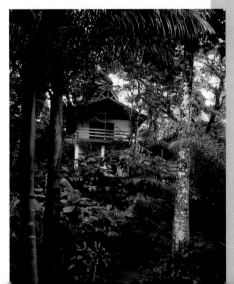

Top Left: Finca Rosa Blanca Country Inn
Right: great for wildlife watching

Two-story beachfront units, each with kitchen, living area, terrace and barbecue. Set in a private 40-hectare (100-acre) reserve on a lovely beach. Easy to arrange snorkeling, riding, fishing and diving. $$$$

Guanacaste

Capitán Suizo
Playa Tamarindo
Tel: 653-0075; Fax: 653-0292
Email: capsuizo@racsa.co.cr
Swiss-owned, this elegant resort is right on Tamarindo Beach, with free-form pool and breeze-cooled dining room. Cool and spacious two-story rooms set in mature tropical garden plus private pool-side bungalows with luxurious bathrooms. Reservations essential in high season as this is one of the most popular hotels in the region. $$$$

Lagarta Lodge Biological Reserve
Nosara
Tel/fax: 682-0035
www.lagartalodge.com
High on a hill overlooking Ostional National Park and the ocean, this Swiss-owned eco-lodge has comfortable rooms with a view and a network of hiking trails in its own riverside reserve. $$

Hotel Las Tortugas
Playa Grande
Tel/fax: 653-0458
Email: surfegg@cool.co.cr
Turtle-friendly hotel on a wide, long, and beautiful beach. Conservationist management. Good restaurant and pool, with excellent surfing opportunities directly in front of the hotel. $$$–$$$$

El Ocotal Resort
Playa Ocotal

Tel: 670-0321; Fax: 670-0083
www.ocotalresort.com
Elegant and secluded hotel on a cliff with spectacular views over the ocean and beach. Rooms and bungalows, some with ocean views and jacuzzis. Swimming pool, tennis, fishing, sailing and dive packages are available. $$$$

Paradisus Playa Conchal Beach & Golf Resort
Playa Conchal
Tel: 654-4123; Fax: 654-4181
www.solmelia.com
The most luxurious and largest resort in Costa Rica, with golf course, tennis courts, and an enormous pool, yet not too obtrusive. It is also close to one of the best beaches in Guanacaste. $$$$

Punta Islita Hotel
Punta Islita, Nicoya
Tel: 661-3332; Fax: 661-4043
www.hotelpuntaislita.com
Part of the Small Luxury Hotels of the World group, perched on a hill overlooking Punta Islita and the Pacific Ocean and one of Costa Rica's most romantic retreats. Luxurious private *casitas* with plunge pools and suites with jacuzzis are dotted over a forested hillside. Superb open-air restaurant and pool overlooking a beach that can be reached by shuttle or a 10-minute walk. Tennis, riding and snorkeling available. Private airstrip. $$$$

Central Pacific

Best Western Jacó Beach
Jacó Beach
Tel: 643-1000; Fax: 643-3246
www.bestwesterncostarica.com
Beachfront hotel with two pools, restaurants and good sports facilities. Rooms are air-conditioned with private balconies. $$$$

Hotel Costa Verde
Manuel Antonio
Tel: 777-0584; Fax: 777-0560
www.costaverde.net
On a lush hillside with great views of Manuel Antonio Park. Monkeys abound around the two cliff-side pools. Comfortable rooms; good restaurant. (Some roadnoise in rooms at top of hotel.) $$$–$$$$

Left: a room with a view
Top Right: El Ocotal Hotel

Nature's Beachfront Aparthotel
Tel: 777-1473; Fax: 777-1475
www.maqbeach.com/natures.html
Right on the beach, pleasant small apartments with kitchenettes and one luxurious, fully equipped, large 'penthouse' apartment. Ocean views and breezes, plus nearby mangrove filled with birds and monkeys. $$-$$$$

Hotel Poseidon
Jacó
Tel: 643-1642; Fax: 643-3558
www.hotel-poseidon.com
An oasis of calm in chaotic Jacó, a small hotel with simple, clean rooms and an excellent restaurant with huge portions of Asian-influenced fish and seafood served in a romantic ambiance. $$-$$$

Sí Como No
Manuel Antonio
Tel: 777-0777; Fax: 777-1093
www.sicomono.com
An environmentally friendly resort, designed to blend in with its natural surroundings. Award-winning architectural design, swimming pool with slide and swim-up bar, Jacuzzi and alfresco grill, and elegant poolside restaurant. Nature trails and free shuttle service to the nearby beach and national park. New butterfly garden. Highly recommended. $$$$

Villa Caletas
Punta Leona, near Jacó
Tel: 637-0606; Fax: 637-0404
www.hotelvillacaletas.com
Only minutes from the beaches of Herradura and Punta Leona, Villa Caletas is set high on a cliff with sweeping views of the Pacific. A French colonial-style mansion with luxurious rooms, free-form infinity pool, fragrant gardens, Greek-style amphitheater with sunset concerts and two open-air bar/restaurants. $$$$

The South

Albergue de Montaña Savegre
San Gerardo de Dota
Tel: 740-1028; Fax: 740-1027
www.savegre.co.cr
Thirty comfortable cabins with private showers and porches on the Chacón family farm in the cloud forests of San Gerardo. Rates include meals, wonderful hiking/birding trails and expert naturalist guides. $$-$$$

Casa Corcovado Jungle Lodge
Nr Playa San Josécito
Tel: 256-3181; Fax: 256-7409
www.casacorcovado.com
A 69-hectare (170-acre) private reserve bordering Corocovado National Park, high on a hill above a surf-splashed beach. Luxurious, breeze-cooled bungalows with stained-glass windows; two spring-fed pools and excellent restaurant. Resident naturalist guides lead trips on park trails and to Caño Island. $$$$

La Paloma Lodge
Drake Bay
Tel: 239-2801; Fax: 239-0954
www.lapalomalodge.com
Pleasant romantic bungalows and rooms built into a lush hillside overlooking the bay. Small pool to practice scuba diving. Good dive packages available. Rates include meals. $$$$

Punta Marenco Lodge
Drake Bay
Tel: 234-1308; Fax: 234-1227
www.corcovadozone.com
Grass-roofed, screened-in huts with verandahs and ocean views from hammocks. Private bath, comfortable beds; family-style meals included. Great hiking trails into rainforest reserve with experienced naturalist guides. $$-$$$

The North

Arenal Volcano Observatory Lodge
La Fortuna area
Tel: 290-7011; Fax: 290-8427
www.arenal-observatory.co.cr
Originally a research station and the only lodge within the park, this forest lodge is the best place for volcano-viewing. The more expensive rooms have picture windows with volcano views. Lots of observation decks and trails. Rates include meals. **$$$$**

Hotel Los Lagos
La Fortuna area
Tel: 479-8000; Fax: 479-8009
www.hotelloslagos.com
Pleasant white *cabinas* and great volcano views. Pool and footpaths. **$$–$$$**

Montaña de Fuego Resort & Spa
Near La Fortuna
Tel: 460-1220; Fax: 460-1455
www.montanadefuego.com
At the base of Arenal Volcano with 50 wooden cabins, each with terrace and volcano view. Bar and restaurant; spa. **$$$$**

Monteverde Lodge
Monteverde
Tel: 645-5057; Fax: 645-5126
www.costaricaexpeditions.com
Comfortable eco-friendly lodge 5km (3 miles) from Monteverde reserve southwest of Arenal, and the most comfortable base for exploring the cloud forest reserve. Spacious rooms with garden or forest views. Restaurant, bar, jacuzzi and tropical gardens. **$$$$**

Rock River Lodge
Tilarán
Tel/fax: 692-1180
www.rockriverlodge.com
Small rustic lodge set above the lake offering excellent activities, including sailboarding, mountain-biking, hiking and horseback-riding. **$$–$$$**

Tabacón Resort
Lake Arenal
Tel: 256-1500; Fax: 221-3075
www.tabacon.com
Part of the Tabacón Hot Springs Resort, this hotel has spacious rooms, some designed for guests with disabilities. There are good volcano views, and hot and cold pools. The resort is within walking distance of the springs. **$$$$**

HEALTH AND EMERGENCIES

Hygiene/General Health
The standard of Costa Rican health care ranks near to that in the USA, Canada and other First World nations, especially in its private hospitals and clinics, which are often staffed by doctors trained in the USA and Europe. Costa Rican dentists also provide competent, inexpensive treatment.

Water in San José and Central Valley is treated. It is, with some exceptions, potable throughout the country.

Medical/Dental Services
For emergency ambulance service in the Central Valley, tel: **911**.

The following are excellent, private medical centers within the Central Valley: **Catholic Clinic** (tel: 283-6166, fax: 283-6171, www.clinicacatolica.com); **Santa Rita Clinic** – maternity and gynecology (tel: 221-6433; fax: 225-1248); **Clinica Biblica** (tel: 257-5252; fax: 255-4947, www.clinica biblica.com) has a recommended emergency treatment room; **CIMA** (tel: 208-1000, www. hospitalsanjose.net) is the newest, full-service hospital in Central Valley, in the western suburb of Guachipélin de Escazú.

For emergency dental care, contact: 800-DENTIST (800/336-8478) for countrywide access to English-speaking dentists.

Outside the Central Valley, ask the manager of your hotel for details of medical centers. English-speaking doctors and dentists also advertize in *The Tico Times*.

Pharmacies
There are good-quality pharmacies throughout the Central Valley. Along the coast and in the mountains, however, there are very few.

CRIME/TROUBLE

Pickpocketing, chain- and watch-snatching, backpack-grabbing and other such forms of theft have become a growing problem, especially in San José. You should feel more relaxed if you take a few common-sense precautions: don't carry valuables (jewelry, watches, cameras, sunglasses, electrical goods or extra cash) with you when you are out on the street and leave backpacks and wallets at your hotel.

When driving through the city, keep your windows rolled up; always lock your car and never leave items visible inside. Do not assume that items in the trunk are safe. Do not leave belongings unattended at the beach.

COMMUNICATIONS AND NEWS

Mail
The central post office is located in San José at Calle 2, Avenidas 1–3. Costa Rican postal services are generally slow. Avoid receiving packages by mail while in Costa Rica. Outrageous duties are sometimes levied on incoming goods and you can spend a day trying to get packages out of customs.

Telephones
The international dialing code for Costa Rica is 506. The country has excellent telecommunications. For information and local directory assistance call 113 and for international information call 124. Phone cards are popular but certain cards work only with certain phones. Email is easily sent and received here, and there are cybercafés all over San José and major tourist destinations.

Television
There is both cable and satellite TV with access to hundreds of stations, many of them in English.

Radio
The only all-English radio station is 107.9 FM, which plays classic rock and has BBC news at 6am, 8am and 5pm. Radio Dos (99.5 FM) has an English program from 6–8am.

The Press
The English-language newspaper *The Tico Times* is published weekly as well as daily, in an on-line version at www.ticotimes.net.

A.M. Costa Rica (www.amcostarica.com) also has daily news and stories on-line. There are also numerous Spanish-language daily newspapers, including *La Nación, La República* and *La Prensa Libre*.

USEFUL INFORMATION

Bookshops
Librería Internacional
Branches in Barrio Dent, Escazú, Multiplaza, Rohrmoser, Alajuela and Zapote
English, French, German, and Italian books, plus Latin American authors in original and translation. Multilingual staff.

7th Street Books
Calle 7, Avenida Central
Tel: 256-8251
This is the best-known English-language bookstore in San José with lots of local lore and naturalist guidebooks. The owners are welcoming and helpful.

Mora Books
Omni Building, downtown San José
Tel: 255-4136
Large selection of used books in English plus bulletin board with local and tourist information.

Papyrus
Next to Mas x Menos supermarket at the end of Paseo Colón, just off Calle 42.

Right: Costa Rica calling

Newspapers and magazines from around the world. Some best-selling paperbacks.

Casa de las Revistas
Calle 5, across from Parque Morazan
International newspapers and magazines.

ATTRACTIONS

Museums
Caribbean Conservation Center
Tortuguero
Tel: 710-0547
www.cccturtle.org
Teaches about the wildlife of the area. Books are on sale; *The Windward Road* by Archie Carr, whose work is largely responsible for the founding of the park at Tortuguero, is recommended. This is also a good place to purchase color plates of the birds of Costa Rica.

Children's Museum
End of Calle 4, downtown San José
Tel: 258-4929
www.cccc.ed.cr
Interactive exhibits on science and natural history in castle-like former prison.

Gold Museum *(Museo de Oro)*
Below the Plaza de la Cultura
Calle 5, Avenida Central, San José
Tel: 243-4202
www.museodelbancocentral.org
An impressive display of pre-Columbian gold jewelry and artifacts. Open Tues–Sun 10am–4.30pm.

Jade Museum *(Museo de Jade)*
11th Floor of the INS Building
Calle 9, Avenida 7, San José
Tel: 287-6034
A world-class collection of pre-Columbian jade pieces, some of which have mysterious origins. On clear days, there are wonderful city views, too. Open Mon–Fri 8.30am–3.30pm.

Museum of Costa Rican Art
(Museo de Arte Costarricense)
Sabana Este at Paseo Colón, San José
Tel: 222-7155
www.crc.co.cr/musarco
Permanent collection and hanging exhibits of paintings and sculpture by 19th- and 20th-century Costa Rican artists. Open Tues–Sun 10am–4pm; admission free on Sun 10am–2pm.

National Museum *(Museo Nacional)*
Calle 17, Avenida Central, San José
(100 meters/yds south of Parque Nacional)
Tel: 257-1433
www.museocostarica.com
Housed in the old Bellavista fortress, which still bears bullet marks from the civil war. General overview of Costa Rica's history with displays from the pre-Columbian and colonial eras. New butterfly garden plus natural history and art exhibits. Open Tues–Sun 8am–4.30pm.

Gardens
Lankester Botanical Gardens
Paraíso de Cartago
Tel: 552-3247
Offers more than 240 hectares (650 acres) of gardens and forest and over 800 species of orchids. Best months to visit are Feb–Apr. Open daily 8.30am–4.30pm. Guided tours available.

INBIOPark
Santo Domingo, near Heredia
Tel: 244-4730
www.inbio.ac.cr
A sampling of all of the country's ecosystems and a snapshot of the national parks in a huge park with live animal exhibits, interpretive trails, video presentations and interesting ecological exhibits. Lakeside

Above: local gossip

café, excellent Heliconia Restaurant, sculpture garden and large souvenir shop.

Arenal Botanical Gardens
Nuevo Arenal
Tel: 694-4305
www.junglegold.com
Botanical gardens founded in 1991. Over 1,200 varieties of tropical plants and attractive trails, plus a butterfly farm. Open daily 9am–4pm; closed Sun May–Oct.

Tours
Café Britt's Coffee Tour
Heredia
Tel:260-2748
www.coffeetour.com
Coffee plantation with an entertaining guided tour. Learn about the history of coffee before a tasting session. A Café Britt bus picks up visitors from the main San José hotels – check with the manager.

WILDLIFE & ECOTOURISM

Only two-thirds the size of Scotland and representing only 0.01 percent of the world's surface, the tiny country of Costa Rica is home to 12 tropical life zones containing an amazing 6 percent of the world's scientifically described flora and fauna.

In total there are about 13,000 plant species, including more than 1,000 species of orchids, 205 species of mammals, 850 species of birds, 220 types of reptiles, 160 varieties of amphibians, and 1,600 species of fresh- and salt-water fish. Costa Ricans have preserved this invaluable biodiversity in protected areas covering more than 25 percent of the national territory, and the country has often been cited as a model for conservation and the birthplace of ecotourism.

However, the destination is in many ways a victim of its own success with many less scrupulous tour operators jumping on the ecotourism bandwagon, and investors and international chains trying to cash in by expanding mass tourism, which brings its own environmental problems. In addition, as admirable as Costa Rica's conservation initiatives may be, the country still faces the inevitable conflict between conservation and consumption and the threat of deforestation, which leads to soil erosion.

As the debate continues between politicians, journalists, scientists, environmentalists and various sectors of the tourism industry, many international non-profit groups and foundations have come to Costa Rica to assist the government in the protection of Costa Rica's invaluable natural wealth.

Many of the tour operators and travel companies recommended in this book have evolved a responsible attitude to business practices and sustainable tourism by using local guides and working with local communities in a sensitive way, controlling numbers of visitors to areas of natural beauty, discouraging unnatural interaction with the wildlife, and promoting small eco-lodges made from natural products rather than large resorts. The cost for these eco-friendly experiences may be higher than traditional tours and hotels but is outweighed by the benefit of supporting and conserving one of the planet's most important wildlife habitats.

Bird Watching

Despite its small size, Costa Rica has roughly the same number of birds as the whole of North America and significantly more than Europe or Australia. Its incredible diversity, with more than 850 species recorded, is partly explained by its many habitats, tropical location and its position on one of the world's great bird migration routes. An excellent field book is *A Guide to the Birds of Costa Rica* by F. Gary Stiles and Alexander Skutch, published by Cornell University Press, 1989.

Top birding destinations are:
La Selva, near Puerto Viejo de Sarapiquí in the northern lowlands, where it is possible to see more than 400 species in a variety of habitats. Contact La Selva Biological Research station through the Organization for Tropical Studies, www.ots.ac.cr.
Tortuguero National Park *(see itinerary 6, page 36)*, home to more than 400 species of bird, including the Great Green Macaw.
Caño Negro Wildlife Refuge *(see itinerary 15, page 56)* for waterfowl, including the Oliveaceous Cormorant and Jabirú stork.
Carara Biological Reserve, near Jacó on the central Pacific coast, is world-renowned for its scarlet macaws.

Cerro de la Muerte *(see itinerary 11, page 48)*, in search of the resplendent quetzal.

Frog Watching

In Costa Rica there are around 160 species of amphibians, including poison-dart frogs, gaudy leaf frogs and glass frogs. The best way to see frogs is to employ a guide who will know where their favorite hiding-places are. On your own, walk quietly and look at moist leaf litter, decomposing trees and large-leaved plants such as philodendrons. Areas around streams, lakes and marshes also tend to have large populations and they are easier to see during dawn and dusk. Frogs are more easily seen during the rainy season (May–Nov) when they lay and fertilize their eggs.

The top frog-watching destinations are:
La Selva Biological Station *(see bird-watching section, page 89)*
Tortuguero National Park
Rincón de la Vieja National Park
Carara Biological Reserve
Corcovado National Park.

For national parks information, visit www.sinac.go.cr.

Monkey Watching

Home to four different species of primates, Costa Rica is an excellent place to watch monkeys. The tiny squirrel monkey is the smallest and rarest species and exists in the south Pacific coastal rainforest, especially in Corcovado and Manuel Antonio national parks. The easily spotted white-faced Capuchin monkeys are widespread throughout the country and, like squirrel monkeys, travel in groups foraging for fruit and insects. Spider monkeys have long thin limbs and tail and rarely come down to the ground. They are most easily observed along the waterways of Tortuguero. Howler monkeys are named after their strange lion-like roar and are often heard around dawn and dusk or when their territory is threatened. They can be found in Tortuguero and the dry forests of Guanacaste and the Nicoya Peninsula.

The best time to see monkeys is early morning and mid-afternoon, when family troops are on the move in search of food.

Turtle Watching

There are few better places in the world than Costa Rica to observe sea turtles nesting. Home to the Green, Hawksbill, Olive Ridley, Leatherback and Loggerhead turtles, Costa Rica has since 1954 pioneered turtle conservation. As noise and light can confuse and frighten the turtles and cause them to return to the sea without laying eggs, it is vital to visit the nesting sites with a proper guide and obey the strict regulations in place to protect these endangered species. Only one in 1,000 baby turtles will survive to reach adulthood and sea turtles are also threatened by hunting, polluted waters and accidental capture by fishermen. But many former hunters have been re-educated as guides and

there are foundations and eco-friendly operators working to increase the turtle population. For further information, contact the Caribbean Conservation Corporation at www.cccturtle.org.

Green turtles nest along the beaches of Tortuguero from July through October. Leatherbacks nest at Las Baulas Marine National Park from October to March, and from mid-February to April in Tortuguero. Hawksbills and Loggerheads nest along the Caribbean coast from May to September.

As many as 100,000 Olive Ridleys come to nest at the Ostional National Wildlife Refuge and leave more than 10 million eggs. This phenomenon is known as the *arribada* and occurs four to 10 times each year between July and November, usually before a new moon, although lesser numbers can be seen any time during the nesting season.

Above: a hummingbird hovers in the Manuel Antonio National Park *practical information*

USEFUL ADDRESSES

Instituto Costarricense de Turismo *(Costa Rican Tourist Institute)*
Plaza de la Cultura at Calle 5 and Avenida Central, San José
Tel: 223-1733; Fax: 223-5452
www.visitcostarica.com
A toll-free number and bilingual operators are available to those calling from the USA, tel: (1 800) 343-6332.

Fundación de Parques Nacionales
(National Parks Foundation)
Calle 23, Avenida 15, San José
Tel: 257-2239 (8am–4pm)
www.sinac.go.cr.
The National Park Foundation administers the park system. Call them for information and permits. Most permits are also available at the park entrances.

The Tico Times
Tel: 258-1558; Fax: 233-6378
www.ticotimes.net

USEFUL TOUR OPERATORS

The following tour operators are all recommended for general outdoor activities in Costa Rica:
Coast to Coast Adventures
Tel: 280-8054; Fax: 225-6055
www.coasttocoastadventures.com
Adventure tourism and cycling specialists.

Cooprena R.I.
Tel: 248-2538; Fax: 248-1695
www.agroturismo.net
Unique experiences in community-run eco-lodges, farms and indigenous communities all over the country; the organization publishes a guidebook to sustainable tourist destinations.

Costa Rica Expeditions
Tel: 257-0766; Fax: 257-1665
www.costaricaexpeditions.com
Long-established and one of the most professional tour operators, pioneering many ecotourism/adventure tours throughout Costa Rica.

Costa Rica Sun Tours
Tel: 296-7757; Fax: 296-4307
www.crsuntours.com
Customized adventure and eco-tours.

Horizontes Nature Tours
Tel: 222-2022; Fax: 255-4513
www.horizontes.com
Well-known nature and adventure specialist that also caters for families and has been operating for many years.

Swiss Travel
Tel: 282-4898; Fax: 282-4890
www.swisstravelcr.com
Large-scale and customized tours throughout the country.

FURTHER READING

Insight Guide: Costa Rica, Apa Publications, Singapore (2004). Detailed overview and insight into Costa Rican history, culture, and places to visit.

What Happen', A Folk History of Costa Rica's Talamanca Coast, by Paula Palmer, San José Publications in English, San José (1993). The history of Costa Rica's Caribbean coast, told in the words of the area's elders. Available at 7th Street Books.

Costa Rica: A Traveler's Literary Companion, edited by Barbara Ras, Whereabouts Press, 3415 Geary Blvd. #619, San Francisco, CA 94118 (1994). An English translation of 26 stories by Costa Rican writers. Oscar Arias edition available on the Net.

USEFUL WEBSITES

Useful websites include:
www.visitcostarica.com
www.costaricanhotels.com
www.hotels.co.cr
www.ticotimes.net (a useful source for listings and current affairs).
www.costaricamap.com is a good general tourism site with many maps of the country, as well as general information and contact details.

ACKNOWLEDGEMENTS

Photography by	**Glyn Genin** *and*
10, 12T/B,	**Henry C. Genthe**
14B, 15	**Harvey Haber Collection**
Front Cover	**Buddy Mays/Taxi/Getty Images**
Cover Design	**Klaus Geisler**
Cartography	**Maria Randell**

© APA Publications GmbH & Co. Verlag KG Singapore Branch, Singapore

INDEX